Voices

ACKNOWLEDGMENTS

The Pennsylvania Commission for Women (PCW) would like to express their sincere appreciation to designer Kristin Haskins (principal of *keydesign*), photographer Darcy Padilla, and writer Julie Liedman for their total dedication to this project. They are a "dream team." Their time, talent, and above all, consummate professionalism are mirrored in every page of this extraordinary book. Of course, coordination of a book such as this is complicated, and we would like to thank Tiffany Strickler, PCW Deputy Director, and Georgianne Diven Coleman, Governor's Southwest Regional Office Deputy Director, for coordinating the myriad facets of this project, and for demonstrating an infinite attention to detail, not to mention unflappable temperaments. We are also indebted to Betty Tuppeny and her talented staff at Domus Advertising, in particular Megan Parker. Their pro bono support served as a springboard for this book. The Commission is grateful to Gloria Hawkins (*Make-Up by Gloria*), who generously donated her makeup skills to help many of the beautiful women in this book shine in front of the camera. PCW would, in addition, like to thank the Philadelphia Foundation for their support of this book and many of the Commission projects.

PCW would also like to thank a superb selection committee comprised of African American and Latina business and community leaders as well as PCW Commissioners. The level of dedication and time they devoted to this project is a testament to their abiding belief that we lead by example, and that the empowerment of women begins by inspiring young girls to achieve.

Most importantly, we would like to commend the Comcast Foundation for its vision in funding *Voices*. From the very beginning, from the first germination of an idea about this kind of role model book, the Foundation was on board and fully engaged, understanding the critical need for race- and gender-matched role models for African American and Latina girls.

Finally, this book would not be possible without Governor Edward G. Rendell who genuinely cares about women's issues and makes them a priority. For that, the Commission is very grateful.

VOICES

AFRICAN AMERICAN AND LATINA WOMEN SHARE THEIR STORIES OF SUCCESS

a publication of the

PENNSYLVANIA COMMISSION FOR WOMEN

HARROWOOD BOOKS

First published in the United States of America in 2006 by
Harrowood Books, 3943 N. Providence Rd., Newtown Square, PA 19073

Copyright @ 2006 for photographs appearing in this book by Darcy Padilla
Photographs appearing as art work on pages 8, 10, 12, 14, 16, 18, 20, 22, 24, 26, 28, 30, 32, 34, 36, 38, 40, 42, 44, 46, 48, 50, 52, 54, 56, 58, 60, 62, 64, 66, 68, 70, 72, 74, 76, 78, 80, 82, 84, 86, 88, 90, 92, 94, 96, 98, 100, 101, 102, 104 and 106 are courtesy of the featured role models.

ISBN-13   978-0-915180-39-4
ISBN-10   0-915180-39-1

Library of Congress Cataloging-in-Publication Data

Voices : African American and Latina women share their stories of success.
    p. cm.
"A publication of the Pennsylvania Commission for Women."
 ISBN 0-915180-39-1
 1. Minority women in the professions--Pennsylvania. 2. African American women--Employment--Pennsylvania. 3. Hispanic American women--Employment--Pennsylvania. 4. Success.
I. Pennsylvania. Commission for Women.
  HD6054.2.U62P468 2006
  650.1092'3960730748--dc22
                      2006022960

PENNSYLVANIA
COMMISSION FOR WOMEN

PRINTED IN THE UNITED STATES OF AMERICA

10 9 8 7 6 5 4 3 2

FOREWORD

Dear Friends,

The future of Pennsylvania lies with its young people, and it is incumbent on us to open doors of possibility for them. Our children need to be encouraged to dream big dreams and to work hard to make those dreams come true.

To that end, role models can help youngsters envision success. The outstanding Pennsylvania women profiled in this book do just that. Their stories combat stereotypical images and communicate information about the work needed to prepare for a future of excellence.

To be a role model, to help children achieve excellence, is to touch the future in the most profound way possible. This book will help shape the potential accomplishments of others—people whose impact may stretch well beyond our own.

I commend the Pennsylvania Commission for Women for its insight in marshaling this project, and all of the women profiled, who gave so freely of their time and talent to bring it to fruition.

If tomorrow's achievements depend on today's actions, then *Voices* will go a long way to assure that Pennsylvania's future is in very good hands.

Edward G. Rendell
Governor, Commonwealth of Pennsylvania

PREFACE

"The whole point of being alive is to evolve into the complete person you were intended to be."
— **Oprah Winfrey**, Television Talk Show Host and Actress

For more than thirty years, the Pennsylvania Commission for Women has been an important advocate for women and girls in the Commonwealth. Our mission is to identify and advance the diverse needs and interests of Pennsylvania's women and girls; to inform, educate, and advocate for them; and to provide opportunities to empower women and girls to reach their highest potential.

This book, an initiative of the Commission and underwritten by the Comcast Foundation, speaks to our mission of empowerment.

Children learn to grow into adults by modeling what they see. If they see productive adults with qualities of character and integrity with whom they can identify, they will be more likely to grow into such adults themselves.

In addition, a growing body of research shows that young people benefit more from same race and gender-matched role models. They perform better academically, have higher educational or professional goals, view extracurricular activities positively, and develop stronger relationships with their role models. They also are less likely to start using drugs and alcohol, less likely to skip class or school, and less likely to be violent.

Research also indicates that many African American and Latino adolescents lack visible role models more often than other adolescents. But if, as the saying goes, seeing is believing, then African American and Latina girls will be able to imagine what they, themselves, can do in the future by learning what women of color are doing already.

The Commission received nominations for a host of women to be included in this book. All are extraordinary women who excel in everything from medicine and law to industry and education, from communication and technology to entertainment, science, and the non-profit arena.

In this book, we profile fifty. The Commission hopes the stories of what inspired these women to be the people they became will resonate with our young readers, and will motivate them to set—and achieve—high goals for the future.

In short, we hope this book will help each girl who reads it to evolve into the complete person she was intended to be.

— Leslie Stiles
Executive Director
Pennsylvania Commission for Women
April 2006

ROLE MODELS

RENEE AMOORE

I didn't plan any of this. But when people came to me with problems, I found ways to solve them. I saw a need and made it a business. "

— RENEE AMOORE
Founder and President
The Amoore Group, Inc.
King of Prussia

Renee Amoore did not plan the way her life would evolve. Not exactly. But her mother taught her, "If you give, you get." That motto inspires her. Being told she *can't,* spurs her on.

Today, she is president of The Amoore Group, Inc., a conglomerate of four businesses Renee founded to address a variety of needs she felt no one was addressing satisfactorily. But this is not something she ever imagined she would do.

Renee, whose mother was a domestic worker who later became a nurse; and whose father was a milkman, sanitation worker, school bus driver, and owner of a small landscaping business, grew up with her seven sisters in an African American community in Bryn Mawr, on Philadelphia's prestigious Main Line. She was one of only six African Americans in her Haverford High School graduating class. Renee *thought* she wanted to be a nurse. When her guidance counselor told her she couldn't because African Americans weren't nurses, Renee was *sure* that's what she wanted to do.

And she did. She received a nursing degree from Harlem Hospital in New York, and worked with low-income families in the South Bronx. Later, back in the Philadelphia area, she worked as a psychiatric nurse at mental health facilities. These experiences taught Renee a lot about the unique health-care needs of disadvantaged people, and led her to found Amoore Health Systems, which helps people with disabilities get jobs. The company also implements health programs in South Africa.

Like her mother, Renee also became active in community and political affairs. She bucked the naysayers to become the first African American elected to the Upper Merion School Board, and spent four years as its Vice President. A third-generation Republican, she met Tom Ridge by chance—and worked on his successful campaign for Governor of Pennsylvania. She later became the first African American on the Pennsylvania Republican State Committee, and eventually, Deputy Chair of the party, a position she still holds.

Her community and political activities led Renee to found three other businesses: 521 Management, a political consulting company; Ramsey Educational Development Institute, which teaches job-readiness skills; and Liberty Services, which offers construction services.

Although her businesses are wide in scope, they have one thing in common: They help people who need help.

"I didn't plan any of this," Renee says. "But when people came to me with problems, I found ways to solve them. I saw a need and made it a business." In everything she's done, Renee says, "I dreamed—and dreamed *big.*"

And she learned. She especially learned how to react to those who revert to stereotypes or who dismiss a person's dreams because they have low expectations of her. "When somebody like that says 'no,'" Renee counsels, "you say 'yes' if it's something you really want to do."

"**I read a lot of novels, and that made me want to travel.**"

– CHERYL LYNNE AUSTIN
Attorney
Retired Captain U.S. Navy Reserve
Roslyn

As a young girl in Ohio, Cheryl Lynne Austin knew she was different. Different because she wanted to travel. Different because she wanted to go to college. No one in her family—no one in her *neighborhood*—had graduated from college. And no one could afford to travel.

"But I read a lot of novels," Cheryl says, "and that made me want to travel." When she was eleven or twelve, she learned about the extensive traveling a friend's aunt did in the military, and saw that as a way for her to travel, too.

But first, college. To pay for it, she held at least two, and sometimes four, part-time jobs. In her sophomore year, when the Naval Reserve Officers Training Corps (NROTC) opened to women for the first time, Cheryl signed up. She didn't do it for the glory of being one of the first women in ROTC. There was no glory. "They really didn't want us there," she says. But Cheryl needed the stipend that came with being in ROTC.

Cheryl was inducted into the Navy with the rank of Ensign, right out of college. Men *still* didn't want women there. "They really gave us a hard time," she says. "You cannot imagine what it was like." But the Navy gave her the opportunity to travel. "We were allowed to catch any military flight that had a vacancy," she says, "so I was always going somewhere." On one such trip, Cheryl happened to sit next to the Navy Chief of Information at the Pentagon. Soon, she had a job with him. Successfully competing in the male-dominated Navy, she eventually became a Public Affairs Specialist at the Pentagon.

Cheryl left active duty as a Lieutenant after seven years and went back to her hometown in Ohio, where she held several impressive government jobs. She also decided to attend law school at night.

Today, she is an attorney in private practice in Montgomery County, specializing in representing men who fail to pay child support. Her objective is to keep them out of jail, so they can earn enough money to make payments.

Cheryl also joined the Reserves after active duty, and rose to the lofty rank of Captain, before retiring with twenty-four years of service. She laughingly asserts she has led three separate lives. "I don't want to look back someday and say, 'What if…,'" she explains.

"While I feel that motherhood is a noble undertaking, women in the twenty-first century can work to find balance between careers, financial independence, and raising a family."

— JOYCE MARIE RAMOS GOMEZ DE AVILA
Multicultural Affairs Director and Associate Professor
Keystone College
Tobyhanna

Joyce Avila is proud of her accomplishments in business and academia. She is equally proud of her domestic accomplishments.

"My children love and respect themselves, their culture, and education," she says. "They know that an education will give them the opportunity to have a good and productive life. This is something that Latina women did not always embrace. When I was growing up, the expectations were for me to get married and have children."

Born in Brooklyn, New York, Joyce moved at age thirteen with her family to Puerto Rico. "A few years later, my father left home," she says, "and I watched my mother make major adjustments to our lives. My mother had followed the traditional Latina wife-and-mother model. I decided then that it was important for me to be independent and self-sufficient when I grew up, and that meant I needed an education."

After high school, as a first step to independence, Joyce moved back to Brooklyn to live with her grandmother. "The opportunities for college were better there," she explains, "and I was able to learn by watching my grandmother, my role model, how a Latina can encompass the beauty of our culture and live in the USA."

During this time, Joyce married, and soon was the mother of two. Her career advanced, but her marriage did not. As a single mother working on Wall Street, she continued going to college, and after many arduous years of work and night school, received a bachelor's degree.

Joyce moved back to Puerto Rico to give her sons an opportunity to learn the culture and language while they were still young. During that time, she changed professions—from the business world to teaching. She also remarried and had three more children.

Eventually, Joyce and her family returned to the United States, and she brought her cultural ties to the world of learning, becoming an advocate and teacher of bilingual/bicultural education.

Today, besides her responsibilities at Keystone College in La Plume, Joyce runs her own company, Creating and Facilitating Equality (CAFÉ), where she consults and facilitates workshops on diversity across the nation.

"In America, you have an opportunity to select from an array of cultural traditions," Joyce believes. "While I feel that motherhood is a noble undertaking, women in the twenty-first century can work to find balance between careers, financial independence, and raising a family.

"Learn who you are and what you want by getting an education and understanding your culture. Create a life of choices for yourself that will bring pride not only to your family and your cultural heritage, but most importantly to you."

CYNTHIA BALDWIN

> "Prepare yourself by studying hard, and learning about the world beyond your neighborhood. Then, be open to what's coming."
>
> — CYNTHIA A. BALDWIN
> Justice
> Pennsylvania Supreme Court
> Pittsburgh

Cynthia Baldwin—*Justice* Cynthia Baldwin—is only half kidding when she says with a laugh, "I *still* don't know what I want to be when I grow up! The important thing is to be happy," she says. "Careers are evolutionary—sometimes even revolutionary." She should know.

Cynthia was born and raised in McKeesport, to parents who had not completed high school but who taught her that with hard work, she could achieve anything. Cynthia has been a high school teacher, a junior high school counselor, a college instructor, an Assistant Dean, a staff attorney, a Deputy Attorney General, a law Professor, and a Judge—the first female African American Judge on the Allegheny County Court of Common Pleas.

In December 2005, Governor Edward G. Rendell nominated Judge Baldwin to an unexpired term on the Pennsylvania Supreme Court, making Cynthia the second female African American Justice on the state's high court.

"People have to be very open to what's coming," she says. Cynthia always has been open. "I've become things I never dreamed of becoming—things I didn't even know existed when I was younger," she says.

"My father worked in the steel mills, but he managed to send me to Penn State. At the time, I thought, 'How lucky I am to be going to Penn State. I can't think of anything better.' Never in a million years did I ever think that one day I would be Chair of the Board of Trustees at Penn State," she says. "I didn't even know there was a Board of Trustees that ran the university. But here I am. I have gone beyond the dreams I had as a young girl."

She was able to do that, she says, because her parents "refused to accept less than excellence from me," and because she refused to accept any less from herself.

Today, Cynthia tells young people, "It doesn't matter from where you come. What's really important is what's in you and where you are going. You should surround yourself with mentors *now*—teachers, friends, adults—who expect nothing but the best from you. Prepare yourself by studying hard, and learning about the world beyond your neighborhood. Then, be open to what's coming.

"And if you do that, I really think your life will be full and you will be fulfilled."

14

> " **It's okay to try something and then say, 'I don't like it.' The worst thing is to sit on the sidelines and not try.** "

> **– ELVA L. BANKINS**
> Managing Director
> Lee Hecht Harrison
> Berwyn

Elva Bankins and her mother still laugh today about the object of Elva's desire when she was a schoolgirl.

"I talked a lot about wanting to drive a Jaguar XKE," Elva says. "One day, I showed my mother a picture, and she said, 'Oh my gosh. It's only got two seats. What about the rest of your family?' I said, 'That can wait until later. First, I just want to have fun.' It was very telling." Indeed it was.

The oldest of seven children, Elva grew up in the 1950s in Baltimore's inner city. She helped her mother a lot around the house, cooking and ironing and taking care of her siblings. "I thought, 'This can't be all there is to life,'" she says.

Not only did Elva not want to settle down and have a family right away, she didn't even want the kind of career that most women with careers had in those days.

"I always thought it was more fun, more adventurous, to follow the path that people were *not* taking," she says. "Everybody else was becoming a nurse or a secretary or a homemaker. I wanted to wear a suit every day and carry a briefcase.

"Everybody said, 'Oh, Elva, who do you know who's like that?' And they were right. I didn't know anybody like that. I always loved to do things differently." So she did.

Elva became a computer programmer when it was highly unusual and difficult for an African American, much less a female, to work in information technology. Eventually, she became the first African American sales manager for a large firm—and opened its Philadelphia office. Later, she became the first female African American sales person for another firm—and was named "Rookie of the Year" there. Today, she is Managing Director of the Philadelphia office of a large, global company, responsible for new business development, client relations, office operations, and profit and loss.

As she looks back on her impressive rise to the lofty heights of the business world, Elva says, "It's important to stay in touch with the thoughts you had when you were young, the thoughts of who you are and where your interests lie, and not to let anyone talk you out of that.

"Listen to advice, but remember who you are and make decisions for yourself. It's okay to try something and then say, 'I don't like it.' The worst thing is to sit on the sidelines and not try."

SYLVIA BARKSDALE

"**It has been all about having people who believed in me, who pushed me when I needed to be pushed. Those teachers wouldn't let me just get by.**"

— SYLVIA JOYCE BARKSDALE
Associate Professor of Social Work
California University of Pennsylvania
Pittsburgh

When Sylvia Barksdale was in second grade, her teacher told her parents to start saving for college because Sylvia had "what it takes." While they didn't know what college was all about, Sylvia says of her parents, "they valued education, and they decided that they would do whatever it took for me to go to college."

And it wasn't just her parents. "I had some teachers who had been educated in historically black colleges," she says. "They had a different approach with us. They had higher expectations of us.

"It has been all about having people who believed in me, who pushed me when I needed to be pushed. Those teachers wouldn't let me just get by. They made me strive to reach my potential. They demanded things of me. They expected certain things from me." Sylvia strives to do the same for her students.

She worked for many years as a Clinical Social Worker at Children's Hospital of Pittsburgh, where she focused on helping families whose children had sickle cell disease. Later, Sylvia collaborated with a team on the development of programs for the prevention of HIV, especially for

women of color. Now Sylvia is a college professor, committed to preparing the next generation of social workers. As such, she has made significant contributions to her students and to the families and communities they will serve in the future.

In addition to her classroom activities, Sylvia is a member of the university's Commission on the Status of Women and the Women's Consortium, providing a voice for all women, and especially women of color, on campus issues.

Sylvia also mentors young people—men as well as women, white people as well as people of color. "I see mentoring as a natural extension of who I am," she says. She has a lot of advice to offer.

"I tell them they should do everything possible to prepare themselves to be the best that they can be. And I tell them not to blame their shortcomings on others or allow the problems other have with them to be thrust on them.

"I tell them to have integrity in all that they do and to do all with honesty and sincerity. Always take the high ground. Always rise above any obstacles that come their way. And always do what is right."

> ❝**Someone said, 'You can't' and I felt I could, if given the opportunity.**❞

— JOAN MYERS BROWN
Founder
Philadelphia Dance Company
(Philadanco)
Philadelphia

Lord Byron's poetic words, "She walks in beauty like the night…" could easily describe Joan Myers Brown. Her elegant, fluid movements are those of a person who has danced most of her life. But Joan Myers Brown is more than a dancer; she's a living legend and a tireless advocate for discipline, creativity, and excellence.

Ironically, she got into dance in the first place because, as a young African American girl, she felt unwelcome in her high school's ballet club. "That only made me more determined," she says today. "I felt it was a challenge. Someone said, 'You can't' and I felt I could, if given the opportunity. I wasn't going to let someone else decide what I could and couldn't do."

Joan actually wanted to be a painter—she still paints in her spare time—but when her high school gym teacher invited her to join the after-school ballet club, she accepted, despite being the only African American in the class.

It paid off. Receiving a scholarship, Joan studied and danced with the Katherine Dunham School in New York. She later toured with Pearl Bailey and Sammy Davis, Jr.

When she tired of life on the road, Joan came back to Philadelphia to open the Philadelphia School of Dance Arts. After ten years, she founded the internationally acclaimed Philadanco, a modern-dance company grounded in the classics. Joan also founded the International Association of Blacks in Dance and the International Conference of Black Dance Companies, and has convened three International Conferences of Black Dance Companies and facilitated the Smithsonian Institution's Conference of Black Dance Companies. Among her numerous awards and honors, Joan was named one of the "Dance Women Living Legends," an honor bestowed on five pioneering African American women who founded distinguished modern-dance companies in black communities around the country.

When Joan started out, the opportunities for African American dancers were few. "The opportunities still haven't grown as far as the times have grown," she says. "But that's no reason not to try."

Today, Joan insists that her dancers cross all disciplines, from ballet to tap to jazz—and beyond. "I make sure they can do everything," she says. I'm about helping dancers do dancing. I'm about helping people follow their dreams."

"After graduate school, I called home and told my mother that I had signed up for the Peace Corps. My mother reminded me that my siblings were still in college, and told me, 'Your Peace Corps will be right here in Philadelphia.'"

— BLONDELL REYNOLDS BROWN
City Councilwoman
Philadelphia

Graffiti spray-painted on her new house spelled action for Blondell Reynolds Brown and led her to where she is today. Her openness to new opportunities allowed that to happen. It's a thread that runs through the fabric of her life. "This was not part of my plan," she says of her life in politics. "My plan was to become a teacher, and eventually a principal. But I had many detours along the way."

The oldest of seven, Blondell came from what she describes as a "poor but rich background" in West Philadelphia—poor economically but rich with books and love. Blondell earned a bachelor's and master's degree at Penn State, and graduated from the University of Pennsylvania's Community Leadership Program and from the Philadelphia Urban League's Leadership Institute. Currently, she is a fellow with the Robert Wood Johnson Foundation.

True to her original dream, she did become a schoolteacher for a time and, later, an Associate Director of Admissions at Penn State.

But Blondell also was a professional dancer. "After graduate school, I called home and told my mother that I had signed up for the Peace Corps," she recalls. "My mother reminded me that my siblings were still in college, and told me, 'Your Peace Corps will be right here in Philadelphia.'"

So Blondell came back to Philadelphia and was encouraged to audition for the Philadelphia Dance Company, also known as Philadanco. She was accepted, and began performing and traveling with the professional black dance company.

Her life took yet another detour on that fateful day that she found graffiti on her house. "I was furious," she recalls. "I said, 'Who's the neighborhood leader I can turn to for help?' I found out there wasn't anyone. "And so, a community activist was born. Blondell became a Committeeperson, and began volunteering in various political campaigns. She was all set to return to teaching when she was offered the job of Legislative Director for a State Senator.

"It was a wonderful opportunity," she says, "so my plans took another detour." The job sparked Blondell's interest in politics, and she decided to run for City Council. She lost the first time, but won resoundingly the second time.

As a Councilwoman, she steadfastly focuses on issues that matter most to her, especially improving the lives of children and youth, the arts, education, and small business development. Her signature program, the annual "Women Making A Difference Celebration," showcases women's accomplishments and provides a platform for issues related to women-owned businesses.

None of her many accomplishments would have been possible if Blondell hadn't been receptive to new experiences. "You must be open to all of the opportunities that come to you, even those that take you into new or unfamiliar territory," she says. "And recognize that the world has no room for mediocrity. Always make sure excellence is your standard."

ESTHER BUSH

> "I say to the people who are full of excuses, 'So what? Why can't you be the one in your family to change the way everyone looks at work, education, achievement?'"

— ESTHER L. BUSH
President and CEO
Urban League of Pittsburgh
Pittsburgh

Esther Bush is serious when she says, "I failed my way to the top. I will make few mistakes today," she says, "because I made so many in the past."

She is confident and optimistic, Esther Bush. "My cup is always half full," she says.

As head of the Urban League of Pittsburgh, Esther has initiated programs for home ownership, youth development, and adult professional development. She has published a number of books and research papers on issues facing the African American community; and she initiated a charter school that was the first to be accredited in Pittsburgh and the second in the state.

Esther was the first woman Director of the Staten Island and Manhattan branches of the New York Urban League. She also was the first woman President of the Urban League of Greater Hartford before becoming the first woman President in Pittsburgh, the post she has held for more than ten years. But don't get the wrong impression: this woman has not been on an unbroken course to the top.

Back in the eighties, when Esther was working for the National Urban League in New York City, President Reagan cut the funding of the program for which she worked. Suddenly, she was out of a job—and unable to find a new one.

So she started a business in her apartment—Seasonal Accents, which manufactured just one product, a Christmas stocking, in two sizes: small, which she sold to corporations that put their logos on them and handed them out to employees with their bonus checks, and to customers; and large, which she customized and sold to individuals.

"I took something simple and made it complex," she says. "I did serious research, and went up and down the Garment District, talking to manufacturers to get advice."

The business succeeded while it lasted, but fizzled when she got a full-time job. The experience, however, taught Esther something she works hard to convey to the individuals the Urban League helps.

"I tell them they can achieve a dream. I say to the people who are full of excuses, 'So what? Why can't you be the one in your family to change the way everyone looks at work, education, achievement?'

"When I got laid off in New York, my boss said to me, 'I'm so sorry,' and I said, 'Don't be. It was my decision to come here. Yes, I'm concerned about how I'm going to pay my rent. But I'm a survivor.'"

And she was.

And she is.

> "If you can't have hugs and hope at home, it doesn't mean those things can't exist for you."

— MARY VIRGINIA LEFTRIDGE BYRD
Retired Deputy Secretary
Specialized Facilities and Programs
Pennsylvania Department of Corrections
Tumwater, Washington, formerly of Camp Hill

Mary Leftridge Byrd has seen the best of the worst. As a former prison Warden who retired recently as Deputy Secretary of the State Department of Corrections, where she was responsible for two maximum- and two medium-security state prisons, she knows a lot about a lot of criminals.

"What is missing in most," she says, "is affirmation." That feeling of recognition, she believes strongly, breeds a sense of self worth.

Mary uses the plants in her office as an example. "They remind me of people," she says. "I have one plant that looks good, and one that doesn't. That's because I paid more attention to the plant that looks good. Now I've moved the one that doesn't look good to a better place, I'm watering and feeding it, and it's starting to look better. People constantly grow and can change, even in a state prison.

"When my mother passed away, I was Superintendent of a men's prison," she recalls, "and I received 623 handwritten notes from the men in that facility. It reflected the best of the people in that environment." Put simply, those who give, get back.

Mary served for many years as Warden or Superintendent of state correctional institutions in Maryland and Pennsylvania before becoming Deputy Secretary of Pennsylvania's Department of Corrections.

Needless to say, she is tough. She's compassionate, too.

"There's a difference between growing up and being raised," she says. "Anything will grow. Raising is an entirely separate matter."

Mary works to develop character by helping inmates become responsible and accountable for their actions. It all goes back to the way she was treated as a youngster.

"When I was in school, I was told by a counselor that I wasn't bright enough to go to college, so I should learn secretarial skills or bookkeeping," she says. "Later, when I wanted to become a county probation officer, I was told I didn't have the talent or the promise. If I had listened to those 'enlightened' individuals, I wouldn't have moved beyond their limited expectations of me."

But her parents told her otherwise. "They were people of meager means but enormous spirit and hope," she says. Mary did go to college, and later soared to the top of the state corrections system. And while she had the support of her family, she thinks even those who don't, can—and must—find support from others in the community, whether it's from teachers, clergy, friends, or acquaintances.

"If you don't have hugs and hope at home," she says, "it doesn't mean those things can't exist for you. Just find other individuals who have them for you. Sometimes just asking opens the right doors."

> "There's so much more to the world than you can actually see in your own space and time."

— R. YVONNE CAMPOS
Founder and President
Campos, Inc.
Pittsburgh

Like the characters in those early video games, Yvonne Campos has moved up the ladder of success by changing directions after bumping into obstacles.

Yvonne is the Founder and President of Campos, Inc., which began as a market research company with two employees—herself and an assistant—in a small office in the corner of one floor of a building in downtown Pittsburgh. At its peak, the company employed thirty full-time and over fifty part-time staff on four floors of the same building. The business focused on market research with expertise in research design, data collection, recruiting, analysis, and market implications. But the negative impact that the rise of the Internet initially had on the market research industry was devastating. On top of that, the distress that 9/11 created on the economy of the U.S. in general and Pittsburgh in particular provided significant challenges to Yvonne's ability to keep her business intact.

Now, she has restructured the company by streamlining and emphasizing its core talents in order to give it flexibility for growth, and the future looks bright once again.

Strategic thinking—looking to the future, setting goals, and figuring how to achieve them—is what Yvonne has been doing all her life. It's something she learned from her parents. And it's something she believes everyone can, and should, learn to do themselves.

Married at twenty, Yvonne worked her way through school, attending several colleges over seven years because of relocation opportunities. At age twenty-five, she was one of only eight students chosen nationally for a fellowship to the University of Utah's Behavioral Learning Institute, where she began to develop the skill of understanding the behaviors and attitudes of people in the marketplace, which she leveraged into a very successful career in market research. Eventually, Yvonne founded her own company, had two children, and faced a difficult divorce. Through it all, she continued to focus on her children and her business, and found time for extensive community service, including becoming the first female President of the Pittsburgh Downtown Rotary in its eighty-five year history.

"My parents were entrepreneurs before the word was popular," Yvonne says today. "They did things out of necessity. They had jobs, but they were always doing extra things to bring in money. It was all about being creative and moving forward."

A fourth-generation Latina, Yvonne grew up trying to move forward by learning about the world beyond her immediate surroundings.

"There's so much more to the world than you can actually see in your own space and time," she says. "It's a matter of taking advantage of the opportunities that present themselves, not being afraid to venture farther than what's comfortable.

"If you never step out of your neighborhood, how do you know what's there?"

> "**I made a commitment to my daughter when she was five years old to look for ways, as a Latina, to excel and be the best role model I could be.**"

— NANCY CHAVEZ
Deputy Commissioner
Bureau of Commissions, Elections,
and Legislation
Pennsylvania Department of State
Camp Hill

Much of what Nancy Chavez did to advance her career in state government these past twenty-five years was done for the sake of her daughter. "I started my career after I had a child," she says. "I knew I had to be a good role model for her." And she was.

She began her career in state government as a clerk typist—a job, she says, that she neither liked nor at which she was particularly good. While working full-time and raising her daughter alone, she earned an associate degree in accounting from a community college, then earned a bachelor's degree in business management and a master's in public administration, specializing in economic development and planning.

Throughout her impressive career, Nancy has risen higher and higher, holding many important positions in state government. On every rung of the ladder up, she has been noted as a strong advocate and facilitator of programs that support women and minorities in business—truly a remarkable role model for women and especially for her daughter, Randi.

In 2003, Nancy added a new dimension to the work she did on behalf of her daughter. She became a strong and outspoken community activist for victims of domestic violence after Randi was murdered by a hit man hired by her husband.

Her life's journey hasn't been easy. But Nancy has taken what life dealt her and turned challenges into opportunities every step of the way.

"I made a commitment to my daughter when she was five years old to look for ways, as a Latina, to excel and be the best role model I could be," she says today. "I was the first of the four girls in my family to go to college. Both of my parents taught me to be independent, although breaking away was hard. But I made a commitment and persevered."

It took fifteen years of going to school at night and sacrificing things in her life until, finally, Nancy Chavez got the degrees she wanted. "Short-term goals are easy to achieve, and they're rewarding," she says philosophically. "But long-term goals are harder.

"You need to set goals and understand what you have to do to reach them. Sometimes it means putting things down on paper. I always write the pros and cons down. It helps me meet my objectives.

"God did a lot in my life to direct me. But when opportunities arose, I took them."

30

"I always said I wanted to be whatever I was interested in at the time. It changed a lot. I wanted to be a geologist and a veterinarian and a rodeo rider. And my parents always said, 'Yes, you can do that.'"

— RENEE CHENAULT-FATTAH
Co-Anchor
NBC News 10
Philadelphia

Renee Chenault-Fattah's parents always were supportive when she told them what she wanted to be when she grew up. Even when she wanted to be a professional rodeo rider.

"I always said I wanted to be whatever I was interested in at the time," she says. "It changed a lot. I wanted to be a geologist and a veterinarian and a rodeo rider. And my parents always said, 'Yes, you can do that.' But they always told me that whatever I did, make sure it does something for someone else." So it wasn't all that surprising when Renee decided to become a lawyer.

"I grew up in the sixties, when the civil rights movement was just coming into being," she says. "The laws were changing. I saw becoming a lawyer as a way I could make a difference in people's lives."

Renee did become a lawyer, and practiced law for a total of four years, including two years in Detroit, as Clerk for Federal Appeals Court Judge Damon J Keith, one of the highest ranking African American judges in the nation, and two years in New York City. While still practicing law, she decided to switch to broadcast journalism. It was a rather large leap, and she didn't quite know how to do it. So she called Norma Quarles, an NBC correspondent whom Renee admired, and asked if the newswoman would talk to her.

"Not only was she willing to talk to me," Renee says, "she invited me to come to the NBC studio. She let me get in front of the camera. I used the tape we made that day to audition for jobs." The veteran newswoman's kindness impressed Renee then—and inspires her today.

"She didn't have to do that," she says. "Now, whenever young people call me, I remember that someone took the time for me, so in turn, I do it for others."

On her way to the top of her field in the Philadelphia market, Renee was a general assignment reporter for the NBC station in Atlanta, Georgia; was a science correspondent for the Fox Network; and was a noon anchor and reporter in Albany, New York. She started her broadcast career at the New Jersey Network.

Although she has been honored many times for her civic and professional contributions, she says she feels *most* honored when young people ask her for advice.

"I know how tough it is for a young person to call a stranger, a grown-up, especially someone famous or someone you admire," she says. "It takes a lot of guts, and I appreciate it for that reason."

What does she tell them? "I tell them no matter how far-fetched their dreams might seem, they shouldn't worry. Go after what you want."

PATRICIA COULTER

> " **You don't have to know exactly where you're going. You just have to start walking.** "
>
> – PATRICIA A. COULTER
> President and CEO
> Urban League of Philadelphia
> Philadelphia

It's a funny thing about Patricia Coulter. She has spent most of her professional life helping people plan their careers. But her own career was completely unplanned.

"My career was never something I set down on paper," she admits. "I thought I wanted to be a teacher, and for many years, I taught elementary school music. I thought, 'This is nice, but I think there's something else I want to do,' although I wasn't sure what that was."

Patricia went back to school, got a master's degree in education, and returned to teaching, but soon realized many of her skills and strengths could transfer into non-teaching jobs.

What ensued were jobs in the public and private sectors—from academia to Fortune 500 companies—where she held leadership positions in general management, business development, executive coaching, management development, and college administration.

Today, she heads the Urban League of Philadelphia, a community-based organization dedicated to empowering African Americans to achieve social and economic equality.

"Although my career path has been winding and indirect," she says, "the one thing that has been there the whole time is the eagerness to challenge myself with one more thing. I've always tried to push beyond my comfort zone.

"As I see it, you can master what you're doing and do more or, as in my case, you can try new things and see if you can step up to something different."

If truth be told, Patricia's earliest plan was to get married and have a husband take care of her, but her father told her not to count on it. "I owe that to my dad," she says. "He said, 'Of course I want you to get married and have children, but I want you to get a good education so you can do for yourself.' And as it turned out, he was right. I have had to do for myself—and raise a child."

Today, Patricia has advice of her own for her child about planning for the future. "My son and his classmates were so concerned about what they were going to do when they graduated, and I kept saying, 'Will you guys relax? It doesn't really matter. All you need to do is get started in something and let that something direct you to something else.' You don't have to know exactly where you're going. You just have to start walking."

PAMELA CRAWLEY

Sometimes, says Pamela Crawley, the big problems we face in life are actually our biggest opportunities for growth. "The events of our lives that we are sure will overwhelm us, are actually the things that make us strong and resilient. It doesn't matter what you choose to do in life, whether you want to be an artist, or a mother, or an executive. With every choice, you are going to be faced with challenges, and how you deal with them helps you become a contributor to the world."

Pamela grew up in a Bucks County community that was not at all diverse. She always knew she was different, but felt comfortable in her own shoes.

"Finding your way through a difficult situation, overcoming obstacles, is an amazing confidence builder," she says. "Nothing can defeat you if you are committed to yourself and willing to work for your success. And once you succeed for yourself, you are able to reach out and help others."

Pamela Crawley has lived through some challenging experiences, especially those that took place early in life.

A former broadcast journalist, Pamela has spent more than twenty years in media, community and government affairs, and public relations. In her current position, she is responsible for shaping the public image and community investment focus of Citizens Bank, and has spearheaded neighborhood investment programs in Philadelphia, Pittsburgh, and other cities across the state. Among her community interests, Pamela chairs the Marion Anderson Award in Philadelphia, which honors humanitarians in the arts, and also provides crucial support to high-school-age artists.

"I am interested in young people in particular because I know what it is to struggle with an overwhelming challenge at an early age," says Pamela. "One of the biggest I faced was the loss of my mother to cancer when I was ten years old. As she became ill, I had to assume an adult's role, cleaning the house and taking care of my younger sister and brother. It was a tremendously difficult time, but looking back I know that it helped me grow in strength. My mother was a witness to that growth and before she died she asked my grandmother to keep an eye on my sister and brother, but said that she had no worries about me. I have come to understand that the strength developed during that terribly difficult time has helped with every other challenge of my life.

"I think the biggest lesson I have learned is the necessity and wisdom of connecting with your inner strength and then sharing that strength with everyone you encounter, regardless of race or religion or economic background," she says. "You begin to look outside of yourself to see who needs help around you and you give it. You learn that what we have in common is that we are all faced with challenges. The thing that separates us is how we deal with them."

DEBORAH DAVIS

> "I had a mind-set that the world was larger than my hometown and I wanted to see what it looked like."

— **DEBORAH C. DAVIS**
Manager, Office of Diversity, Inclusion,
and Employment Equity
Penn State Milton S. Hershey Medical Center
Lancaster

Deborah Davis was taught never to talk back to her elders. But she did—big time—when she was sixteen years old. It was one of the best things she ever did. It changed the course of her life.

The daughter of an auto mechanic and a domestic worker, Deborah was in the commercial program in high school at the time. "I was destined to be a secretary," she says. "In my family, that would have been a big step. No one had ever finished high school." But an advertisement for Upward Bound, a federal program that offered assistance and guidance for students, particularly minority students, who wanted to go to college, caught her attention.

"I had a mind-set that the world was larger than my hometown," she says, "and I wanted to see what it looked like. But when I told my guidance counselor I wanted to apply to Upward Bound, she said the program wasn't for me. Somehow, I got up enough gumption to disagree with this older woman."

Deborah did submit an application, was accepted, and went on to college. "Thank goodness I spoke up," she says today.

Deborah earned a degree in sociology, and became the first female African American Juvenile Probation and Parole Officer in Lancaster County. Later, she earned a master's degree and, because she wanted to break the "glass ceiling" at the upper levels of social service agencies, earned a doctorate degree of social work as well. Over the years, she has held a number of important jobs helping the poor and disadvantaged—from counseling young drug and alcohol abusers to helping minority teenagers pursue college educations to helping to foster healthy relationships in the workplace.

Today, in her position as Manager, Office of Diversity, Inclusion, and Employment Equity, Deborah is responsible for ensuring fair employment practices and for implementing diversity and cultural competency training within the medical center. She also is Co-Chair of the Dean's Council on Diversity, which promotes a climate of inclusiveness, acceptance, and respect for faculty, staff, patients, visitors, and the community at large.

Imagine where she would be today if Deborah had listened to her guidance counselor back in high school!

"It's important to listen to advice," Deborah says. "Your parents and teachers have experience at life. At the same time, you have to think about what life will be like for you when you're older. In the end, it's *you* who determines your future."

> "**My music teacher told me, 'I know you are poor, but I know you have talent. If you let me shape you, you can become a great musician. It could be your ticket out of here. It's up to you.'**"
>
> — **MARIA DEL REY**
> Children's recording artist
> and producer
> Hershey

As a poor Cuban refugee in Miami, Maria Del Rey sometimes felt invisible. "Even my parents didn't know how to find a better life for me outside of the barrio," she says.

But things changed in fifth grade. "My music teacher told me, 'I know you are poor, but I know you have talent. If you let me shape you, you can become a great musician. It could be your ticket out of here. It's up to you.'"

"By seventh grade, I knew I had a gift. Other people couldn't play and hear music the way I did," she says. "Of course, a lot of people have a gift but do nothing with it."

Maria did something with her gift. "I held on to that gift like it was a lifeline," she says. "I immersed myself in it. I always felt like I was in a bubble of grace with that immersion."

By the time she was eighteen, Maria was playing the cello with the Miami Philharmonic. She won a scholarship to college and was the first woman in her family to be college educated.

After graduating, Maria moved to Los Angeles and turned to singing. Her voice sold billions of dollars' worth of products through worldwide bilingual advertisements. She also was an independent vocal contractor, negotiating union contracts, prices, and terms between record labels and musicians, singers, producers, and talent agents.

Today, Maria lives with her husband and son in Hershey, and is recognized as one of the top bilingual children's producer/artists in the Americas, focusing on educational bilingual music that breaks down the barriers between Latino and non-Latino children. She has been nominated for a Latin Grammy and several Parents' Choice awards. Her latest venture is producing non-violent action and adventure films for families.

Maria says an important lesson she learned about herself—and other Latinas—fuels her drive. It happened shortly after her college graduation, when she entered a bike race on Mackinac Island in Michigan. Although she wasn't particularly athletic, and although one of the other participants was an Olympic hopeful, Maria trained hard. By the mid point of the race, she was in third place when, incredibly, the lead competitor's bike chain broke, and the next competitor fell off her bike. Suddenly, the championship was within Maria's reach.

"I could have taken it," she says, "but I didn't. I didn't believe I deserved it." Maria came in third, losing by two seconds. "That's how a lot of young Latina girls feel. They think they only deserve third best. I learned a huge lesson that day. Not that I have to win or else—but that I'm as worthy of number one as anyone."

PATRICIA DOCUMÉT

I talk with an accent, so people tend to think I am stupid. They don't always take me seriously, or they fake not being able to understand me when they can."

— PATRICIA I. DOCUMÉT

Pediatrician
Coordinator, Doctoral Program and Assistant Professor
Department of Behavioral and Community Health Sciences
Graduate School of Public Health, University of Pittsburgh
Pittsburgh

Patricia Documét was ready to give up medicine the first time one of her patients died. "I was in medical school, and until then we had only worked on cadavers," she recalls. "It's one thing to work with dead bodies. It's another thing to work with people who are alive and then die. I had a patient who was comatose, and she died. I told my professor, 'I can't be a doctor. I can't deal with seeing people die.' He told me, 'It's good you don't like it. It means you care.'"

Patricia Documét cares. And because of that, she pushes herself to do things that are difficult for her.

The daughter of a physician, Patricia was born and raised in Peru, in comfortable surroundings, with a traditional Catholic education. In medical school, and in her work as a pediatrician in Peru, she explored issues that raised questions about some of the beliefs of her traditional medical education, such as the idea that doctors are infallible, or that patients' perspectives were not important in treatment decisions. Her ability to explore other points of view was kindled as a youngster, when Patricia became involved in theater productions in school. From the experience of playing various roles and discussing characters' motivations, she learned to step outside her own feelings in order to see many different views of the same situation. This technique is essential to her research today.

Coming to Pennsylvania so her husband could pursue his work in medical research, Patricia was not able to practice medicine with her Peruvian credentials. Instead, she earned a doctorate in public health. Today, she teaches and advises doctoral students, and conducts research with an eye toward providing better health care for the poor and disadvantaged. She also is involved in community and religious organizations aimed at uniting and aiding the Latino community.

Patricia's research focuses on improving access to health care for Latinos in Southwestern Pennsylvania, but addresses problems encountered throughout the U.S. Her study on the underutilization of breast and cervical cancer testing by minority women, for instance, identified perceptions, expectations, and barriers related to cancer screening among African American, Appalachian, Amish, and Latina women.

In both her professional and community advocacy work, Patricia says she sometimes has to overcome her own reticence to speak up in order to complete the task at hand. "You still have to do those things that scare you," she says. "They might never go away. Control your fear and go and do it. It sounds easy, but it's not.

"Being a Latina, I am treated strangely sometimes. I talk with an accent, so people tend to think I am stupid. They don't always take me seriously, or they fake not being able to understand me when they can. I just tell those people I don't *think* with an accent."

42

WILLA DOSWELL

> "Develop your gift. Whether it's writing, drawing, your voice, or cheerleading, develop your gift—and share it. Then reach back and help a girl younger than you develop hers."
>
> — WILLA M. DOSWELL
> Associate Professor
> University of Pittsburgh
> School of Nursing
> Founder, NIA Project
> Pittsburgh

Most people have something they do well. Willa Doswell sincerely believes this is so. "Develop your gift," she tells young people, especially young African American girls. "Whether it's writing, drawing, your voice, or cheerleading, develop your gift—and share it. Then reach back and help a girl younger than you develop hers."

A nationally recognized nurse, educator, and researcher, Willa has dedicated her professional life to doing just that. As an educator, she reaches back and helps by teaching nursing research and guiding the dissertation research of graduate students. As a nurse, she shares the fruits of her research with young girls in the Pittsburgh area through the NIA Project, which she founded in collaboration with several colleagues at Pitt's School of Nursing. NIA is appropriately named for a principle of Kwanzaa, meaning "sense of purpose." An after-school program, it helps adolescent African American teens and preteens develop knowledge and skills that promote self-esteem, healthy lifestyles, and techniques for making good decisions.

Willa's interest and work in nursing research began shortly after she graduated from nursing school, but it wasn't until many years later, when her own two daughters were facing puberty, that she developed what has become her specialty: early sexual behavior in preteen and early teen African American girls.

Over her academic career, she has delivered hundreds of papers and scholarly presentations at local, national, and international professional meetings. She has served as an international consultant in research to universities in Belgium and Jamaica; has taught nursing research at five colleges and universities; and has mentored scores of minority students.

Willa's research has shown that African American girls tend to mature physically at an earlier age than other ethnic groups. Furthermore, she believes that the popular media has compromised African American girls' identities. Together, these factors create risk behaviors that NIA strives to reverse.

For instance, vehicles like hip-hop videos tend to depict stereotypes of African American women as being flirtatious, wearing skimpy clothes, and acting subservient to men. This, she believes, influences girls to act and dress that way, and implies those behaviors will help them attract men. Willa is dedicated to changing those perceptions.

"We tell the girls: 'See yourself as beautiful; develop your talents; and be aware of the messages you send with the way you act and dress. Don't let anybody define you. And don't let anybody put you down.'"

"**My shyness was standing in the way of things I wanted to do—like stand up in front of the class. I knew my shyness would hold me back in life. I was 12 and I remember thinking, 'I need to work on this.'**"

— SHEILA DOW-FORD
Executive Vice President and Chief Counsel
Pennsylvania Higher Education Assistance Agency
Harrisburg

When she was just twelve years old, Sheila Dow-Ford would look in the mirror and wonder who she was. "I'm really a Barbara or a Veronica," she would say. "I'm not a Sheila.

"I was trying on identities," she explains. "I was asking, 'Who am I? Where do I fit in this world?' It helped me define my relationship with the larger world. You can do that at that age. You can create your own space."

That is precisely what Sheila Dow-Ford did. An attorney, she is Executive Vice President and Chief Counsel of the Pennsylvania Higher Education Assistance Agency (PHEAA), one of the largest student loan organizations in the nation. Her job is to provide legal and business guidance to all parts of the agency, which has $45 billion in assets and over two thousand employees in seven states, Puerto Rico, and the Dominican Republic.

It's a very responsible and high-profile job for someone who says she was practically paralyzed by shyness when she was a youngster.

"My shyness was standing in the way of things I wanted to do—like stand up in front of the class," she says. "And I knew my shyness would hold me back in life. I was twelve and I remember thinking, 'I need to work on this.'"

The way twelve-year-old Sheila "worked on" her shyness was to run for student government.

"It was hard," she says. "I had to struggle against my natural tendencies." But it was worth it.

Sheila was elected President of her sixth-grade class. The experience taught her that "you have to be able to visualize what you want. I ran, understanding that I wanted to win," she says.

The experience also taught her that "you have to dare to dream, and challenge yourself to do something that would take you out of your comfort zone." To do that, "it's important to study people you admire.

"Find the strengths, characteristics, and qualities within people you look up to," she adds. "Maybe someone has strength of character, or the ability to speak well, or is very disciplined about a particular part of her life. Think about those qualities you admire, and how you can attain them. It can be your friends. It doesn't mean looking up to someone at such a high level that her qualities are unattainable.

"People think kids can't have philosophical thoughts, but they can. You can think beyond yourself to the larger world."

Sheila did. She dared to dream and to challenge herself. Eventually, she stopped thinking she was a Barbara or a Veronica. Now when she looks in the mirror, she knows exactly who she is.

> "I went to apply for a job at the Post Office, and a man there said to me, 'The police department is going to start hiring broads soon. You have the qualifications. You should apply.'"

— GWENDOLYN J. ELLIOTT
Founder, Gwen's Girls
Retired Police Commander
Pittsburgh

If there's a message Gwen Elliott wants to convey to young girls today, it's that they always have choices in life, and that making the right one can change their lives in a split second. It happened to her. "I went to apply for a job at the Post Office," she says with a chuckle, "and a man there said to me, 'The police department is going to start hiring broads soon. You have the qualifications. You should apply.' I filled out the application, took the test, and scored higher than any other female applicant. When they called me, I had to make the decision right away. I took a risk and it changed my life."

Gwen became one of the first female officers in the Pittsburgh Bureau of Police, and the first woman officer to ride in a car. During a distinguished twenty-six-year career on the force, she also was the first woman to achieve the rank of Sergeant, and the first African American woman to be promoted to Commander.

But police work was only one of Gwen's careers. She served for fifteen years in the military—first in the Air Force, then in the Air National Guard, and then the Army Reserves—enlisting after high school to further her education. While in the military, she got more of an education than she bargained for. Stationed in the South, she experienced racial segregation. And because the armed services had not yet incorporated women into daily military life, she experienced gender segregation as well. "It toughened me up," Gwen maintains, "but it didn't get me down."

After leaving the military, Gwen worked in the mental health field as a Crisis Intervention Counselor. But funding was always precarious and she wanted more stability—which is why she was applying for a job at the Post Office when the prospect of joining the police force was presented to her.

Her work on the force taught Gwen about the plight of the girls and young women who came to the attention of law enforcement officials, and she came to realize that existing services fell short of meeting the gender-specific needs of those at-risk girls. So when she retired from the force, she created Gwen's Girls, which provides a variety of specialized gender-specific, age-appropriate educational, cultural, spiritual, and leadership programs to help eight to eighteen year olds lead productive lives.

"In the inner cities," Gwen says, "the people making the most money are dope dealers. Young girls need to see that lifestyle as unacceptable. We have to show them that if you work hard and get an education, you can find a good, legitimate job; a house in the suburbs; and have a very nice standard of living.

"Girls need to be exposed to what the real world is," she says. "They have to see what the alternatives are."

> "There were a lot of things I wanted to accomplish— and education helped me accomplish them."

— LILLIAN ESCOBAR-HASKINS
Founder, Lead Researcher,
and Senior Partner
Alegre Advertising and Research
Lancaster

According to Lillian Escobar-Haskins, there are Puerto Ricans…and there are Puerto Ricans. "Puerto Ricans born and raised on the island are different from those born and raised here in America," she explains. "Latinos raised in Puerto Rico don't see themselves as a minority. They've never felt marginalized. But those of us born here, who are second generation, we have to live in two worlds. At home, we're very Puerto Rican. Outside of home, we're very American."

Second-generation herself, with parents who knew little about American culture, Lillian says, "I had to learn everything through trial and error." Learn she did.

Lillian has made significant and enduring contributions through her research studies. Many communities have used her findings and analyses to improve the quality of life for Latinos in Pennsylvania. As a long-time activist, Lillian entered the political arena, running for the Pennsylvania Legislature, and powerful force in Lancaster's political and social structure. She later was appointed to head the Governor's Advisory Commission on Latino Affairs. She also is founder of Alegre Research and Design, which focuses on reaching diverse audiences in a culturally relevant manner.

These are remarkable contributions under any circumstances, but they are all the more remarkable because they were made by a person who, when growing up, did not have higher education or a career on her radar screen.

"College was never something that was discussed," she says. "My parents didn't know anything about it, and no school counselor ever talked to me about it. There was never a discussion about higher education options or a career. I was expected to get a job or get married."

But she did go to college—several times. The first time was when the state university system in New York, where she lived, invited her to apply through a civil-rights program that provided special opportunities for people of color. "I wasn't prepared," Lillian says. "I didn't understand how important it was."

Lillian got married, dropped out, and began a family. She tried college again, but with small children, and despite a very helpful and supportive husband, found it to be too much, and she dropped out again. Eventually, she had four children, and she and her husband moved to Lancaster. After eight years as a stay-at-home mom, she found her choices limited when she reentered the workforce. Lillian finally realized that "if I wanted to progress, I needed an education.

"I was thirty-four and had four children when I earned my master's degree. Getting it was one of the best things I ever did.

"I didn't understand the importance of education until later in life," she says. "But there were a lot of things I wanted to accomplish—and education helped me accomplish them."

> "**Don't be intimidated. Speak up when you see an injustice. You can be a part of the process. As my father used to say, 'You grow your own revolution.'**"

— BRENDA L. FRAZIER
Allegheny County Councilwoman
Pittsburgh

When she was elected to the Allegheny County Council in 2001—the first African American female on the fifteen-member body and the first to hold elected office in the county's revamped government—Brenda Frazier said that up until that point, African American women had had no voice in matters that concerned them.

"We were not at the table," she said. "And if you're not at the table, you can't eat." Brenda's at the table now—and she's dishing up programs aimed at righting wrongs and insuring that justice is served. She is Chair of the Health and Human Services Committee, and a member of the Appointment Review, Budget and Finance, Economic Development, Government Relations, and Campaign Reform committees.

While her election brought diversity of thought and experience to the Council—twelve of its fifteen members had been white men until then—her government work was simply a continuation of what she had been doing all her life, and what she was raised to do.

Growing up in segregated public housing, Brenda had been reminded daily of what was wrong with her world. She was taught by her mother, a schoolteacher who was turned away from jobs time after time because of her gender and race, not to bemoan injustice but to go out and do something about it.

An aunt in New Jersey taught her how. "My aunt had a very strong influence on me," Brenda says. "She was active in civil rights, in the anti-lynching movement, and she traveled all over, advocating for the changes she believed in. I saw my aunt face one challenge after another, and I just thought that was the way you live."

That certainly is the way Brenda lives. A former middle school teacher, she has always been active in local civic affairs, participating in projects that addressed issues of concern, especially in the areas of education, health, and racial equality. While on sabbatical from teaching, she worked as a real estate agent—and overcame by a mile the low expectations her colleagues had of African Americans' buying and selling abilities.

Eventually, Brenda's activism began to focus on government, and she worked her way through the political process until she won the coveted Council seat she holds today.

To young people interested in following in her footsteps, Brenda has these words of advice: "Don't be intimidated. Speak up when you see an injustice. You can be a part of the process. As my father used to say, 'You grow your own revolution.' In due course, you'll find people who think the same way you do."

"I've experienced both racial and gender discrimination at times during my career. That is reality. Some situations provide challenges. You can't let them define you, and you can't let them hold you down."

— **PAMELA W. GOLDEN**
Senior Vice President
Communications
Allegheny Conference on
Community Development
Pittsburgh

Although being a female African American communications expert in Pittsburgh is a far cry from being a Prime Minister of England, Pamela Golden and Sir Winston Churchill share a common principle—a commitment to giving back. "Winston Churchill's words, 'We don't make a living by what we get; we make a living by what we give' have become my mantra," Pam explains. It's not just her mantra; it's the way Pam lives.

Throughout her career, Pam has broken through glass ceilings and opened doors for both women and African Americans. In many cases, particularly early in her career, it was not uncommon for her to be the only—and sometimes the first—person of color in mid-management positions or on project teams and committees. As she rose to the top of the communications field, those she has mentored and managed have advanced as well. At every step of the way, Pam has worked to achieve equality, address discrimination, dispel myths grounded in ignorance, and affect an appreciation for the value of diverse perspectives and experiences.

Today, as Senior Vice President for Communications at the Allegheny Conference on Community Development, a private-sector economic-development organization, Pam is responsible for the marketing communications programs and strategies for the organization, which works to improve the business climate of Southwestern Pennsylvania.

It is important work because it concerns the future vitality of the region. Equally important to the future is the work Pam does mentoring young African American women.

"Mentoring is not an option," she says. "It's an obligation. There are lots of women willing to do it. People can be surprisingly approachable, and are willing to help. If you see someone you admire, or someone you respect, you shouldn't hesitate to seek her advice. I am always flattered when I'm asked to be a mentor. It's important to give back. It's a circle in the Universe. Lots of people helped me."

Pam grew up in Pittsburgh—the eighth generation of a family of Pennsylvanians. Her father was a pharmacist and science teacher. Her mother, who grew up in Johnstown, had wanted to be a nurse but couldn't go to nursing school there because of her race. She moved to Pittsburgh, married Pam's father, raised a family, and then went to school and became a nurse. "She showed real determination," says Pam. It's a trait Pam displays, also.

"I've experienced both racial and gender discrimination at times during my career," she says. "That is reality. Some situations provide challenges. You can't let them define you, and you can't let them hold you down. I learned from my mother's fortitude and resolve.

"I expect to continue to face obstacles. It's up to all of us who have made it, men and women alike, to work to break down those barriers."

"To me, success is not measured by the heights obtained, but by the obstacles overcome. Sometimes, we think the only way we can overcome an obstacle is by superhuman effort."

— IVONNE C. GUTIERREZ DE BUCHER
Chief of Staff
Director, Office of Community Services and Advocacy
Pennsylvania Department of Aging
Harrisburg

Many people have a defining moment that colors their outlook on life. Ivonne Bucher's is particularly vivid. "My family and I were flying from California to Taiwan. I was ten and my brother was five," she says. "Suddenly, the engines went out. Everyone was screaming. The oxygen masks came down. We were preparing for a crash landing.

"My mother said to us: 'Guess what. We are going to have the opportunity to jump into the Pacific Ocean and go swimming. We weren't expecting this, but it's going to be great.' We were really excited. We couldn't understand why everyone around us was hysterical.

"Well, we landed in the Philippines, and I can't tell you how disappointed I was that we didn't get to go swimming in the Pacific Ocean. My mother made it sound like so much fun. That's what my parents always did," says Ivonne. "They raised us to believe that every obstacle is just an opportunity waiting to happen." That is the philosophy she has lived by ever since.

A native of Puerto Rico, Ivonne was an "Army brat," traveling to, and living in, many places around the world with her military family. "Wow! We're going to the next place. That's how my parents handled all the moves," she says.

A registered nurse, Ivonne also holds a bachelor's degree, and is pursuing a master's degree, in business administration (MBA). She worked for many years as a nurse before going to work for the Commonwealth of Pennsylvania, where she has held a number of key positions. In August 2002, Ivonne became the highest-ranking Latino in the history of Pennsylvania state government when she became Deputy Secretary of Aging. Currently, as Chief of Staff and Director of the Office of Community Services and Advocacy for the Pennsylvania Department of Aging, she works to ensure that the elderly receive services that allow them to remain safe in their homes and communities by helping them solve problems that come their way.

"To me, success is not measured by the heights obtained, but by the obstacles overcome," Ivonne says. "Sometimes, we think the only way we can overcome an obstacle is by superhuman effort. A small stream is formed by water pushing its way through earth and rock. Picture a large rock in the way of the water. The water does not go through the rock, rather around it, finding its way to the desired destination. Eventually it carves a wider and wider path as the rock and earth give way until eventually you have the Grand Canyon.

"In the very same way, you can carve a path for yourself. It takes time, patience, effort, and determination. But it doesn't take an unusual person."

"When I was in eighth grade, my grandfather said to me, 'You need to fix yourself up or you're not going to be anything in life. You'll just marry a bum and have a house full of kids.' I decided then and there to do whatever I needed to do to prove him wrong."

— LINDA A. HICKS
Chief of Staff
Pennsylvania Department of
Public Welfare
Harrisburg

S ome people are motivated by the inspiring words of a famous person. Linda Hicks was motivated by the disparaging words of her grandfather. "There's one thing that stands out most vividly in my mind. I can remember it to this day," she says. "When I was in eighth grade, my grandfather said to me, 'You need to fix yourself up or you're not going to be anything in life. You'll just marry a bum and have a house full of kids.' I decided then and there to do whatever I needed to do to prove him wrong." She did. And she has. Her only regret is that her grandfather didn't live to see it.

Linda has served the Commonwealth of Pennsylvania for over twenty-seven years, holding a variety of leadership positions. At present, she is Chief of Staff for Secretary of Public Welfare Estelle B. Richman, a position she has held for more than eleven years. She acts on behalf of the Secretary with considerable latitude on operational issues, advises and assists the Secretary, and provides day-to-day oversight of the executive office. Throughout her remarkable service to the Commonwealth, as well as in her volunteer work in the community, Linda has advocated for youth development and helped organizations address issues of marginalized and diverse groups.

Growing up, she was among those marginalized people she works so hard to help today. Linda is the daughter of a domestic worker, a single mother who had to swallow her considerable pride to collect welfare so she could care for her four children. Her mother's plight prompted

Linda to vow early on to beat the odds by doing well in school, going to college, and doing well-paying, productive work.

Although her grandfather's ridicule motivated her in a negative way, Linda says the strongest positive motivating force in her life was her mother.

"She said, 'If you focus on your books, I will back off on household chores. You won't have to clean the house and scrub floors,'" Linda recalls. "I didn't want to be a domestic, and I equated housework with domestics, so I agreed."

Linda did well in school, and went on to graduate from college—the first person in her native Trenton, New Jersey, neighborhood to do so—with the help of a full scholarship from Douglass College.

Although she faced color and gender barriers on her rise through Pennsylvania state government, she says others behind her won't have to as much.

"There are a lot more opportunities today for African American women than there were back then. The ceiling has opened up because of the women who came before," she says. "It's not as big a challenge, because they won't be the first or second. They'll be a lot more comfortable than I was. They'll be able to look around and say, 'I'm not alone.'"

> "Never hesitate to show your intelligence. Be yourself. Don't be afraid to raise your hand when you know the answer."

— CHARISSE LILLIE
Vice President, Human Resources
Comcast Corporation
Senior Vice President, Human Resources
Comcast Cable
Philadelphia

Just who did Charisse Lillie think she was? That's what some of her teachers wanted to know when she was a youngster. Not everyone was partial to smart girls back then.

"I always wanted to be a lawyer," Charisse says. "I grew up in Houston, when Barbara Jordan was a young lawyer in the State Legislature."

Having as your role model the first African American woman to serve in the Texas Legislature and in the U.S. House of Representatives is pretty admirable, one would think.

But Charisse's teachers didn't think so. "I was told in school that girls aren't lawyers," she says. "When I mentioned Barbara Jordan, my teachers would tell me Barbara was just different. Thankfully, I had parents and grandparents and an extended village of supporters who didn't think that way."

Charisse did, indeed, become a lawyer, and embarked on a celebrated and impressive career in both government and the private sector. She clerked for a federal judge in Philadelphia, worked as a civil rights lawyer in Washington, D.C., served as Deputy Director of Community Legal Services in Philadelphia, taught law at Villanova Law School, and served as an Assistant U.S. Attorney and General Counsel to the Philadelphia Redevelopment Authority. In 1990, she became the first African American woman to serve as Philadelphia City Solicitor. A specialist in labor and employment issues, she then went on to chair the Litigation Department of a major Philadelphia law firm before bringing her expertise in labor and management concerns to Comcast.

Clearly, her teachers' lack of support for a smart young girl's lofty ambitions did not deter Charisse. "I remember in middle school, having friends who went into a shell, not wanting to raise their hand and answer questions, just wanting to be invisible," Charisse says. "But my parents and my friends didn't have problems with girls being smart.

"That's why I always tell young girls today: Never hesitate to show your intelligence. Be yourself. Don't be afraid to raise your hand when you know the answer."

Charisse is still friendly with some of the smart girls she went to school with. "It's remarkable to be able to reach back to that part of your history," she says. "Friends are important. You should maintain your friendships, even through the ups and downs.

"Part of the success I had in my law career was as a direct result of the friendships and networks I maintained. I thought I would always be a government lawyer, but because I had maintained contacts with friends who were doing all sorts of things, I found support and help in the second phase of my career in the private sector."

Smart, indeed.

> "I was fascinated and inspired by [my grandmother]…I spent time asking her questions and watching her work on her farm. I didn't know what I was learning from her at the time, but I valued it. I just trusted my instincts."

— ALBA E. MARTINEZ
President and CEO
United Way of Southeastern Pennsylvania
Philadelphia

Alba Martinez says that more than anyone else in her life, her grandmother inspired her when she was a child. Alba didn't know why at the time. Her grandmother just had that effect on her.

"I was fascinated and inspired by her," Alba says. "Although she lived three hours away, I made an effort to get close to her. I spent time asking her questions and watching her work on her farm. I didn't know what I was learning from her at the time, but I valued it. I just trusted my instincts." Her instincts paid off.

"What I learned from my grandmother guided me through my legal practice and government work, and in my personal and political life," Alba says unequivocally.

Alba's career has centered on health and human services, both in the government and non-profit sectors. As head of the United Way of Southeastern Pennsylvania, she is responsible for the organization's day-to-day operations, and oversees its annual fund-raising campaign, which raises $50 million to support over three thousand agencies in the Greater Philadelphia region. That position is the latest and biggest arrow in a quiver of top leadership jobs that included Commissioner of the Philadelphia Department of Human Services, Executive Director of Congreso de Latinos Unidos, Inc., and Managing Attorney of Community Legal Services in Philadelphia.

Although her grandmother never got past the third grade, Alba says her own remarkable success can be attributed in large part to the way her grandmother lived her life.

"I learned from her to be kind, to be generous, to be honest, to be hard working, to be focused, and to sacrifice today to get what you need tomorrow. And most of all," she says, "I learned to think about others even when you are in need of taking care of yourself."

These values served Alba well when she moved to America to attend law school. Although her parents were English professors in Puerto Rico, their instruction was not enough to prepare Alba for the kind of English she would need in an American law school.

"I was an A student in English in Puerto Rico," Alba says, "but I lacked the technical language to manage in school in America. I was at risk of failing out, but I asked for help and got it. Even after I became a lawyer, I needed help and guidance to become an accomplished lawyer. I learned that the hardest part of getting help is asking for it, but once you ask, people usually give it."

Despite her dizzying professional success, Alba says she has asked for, and gotten, help all through her career. "I've had to work hard for every achievement I've reached," she says. "I never felt entitled." Her grandmother taught Alba humility, too.

"**I found reading about, and talking to, male leaders was most helpful. It helped me learn how leadership is developed.**"

– FREDERICA A. MASSIAH-JACKSON
President Judge
Court of Common Pleas
Philadelphia

Even though she went to an all-girls' high school and a women's college, Frederica Massiah-Jackson always studied the lives of successful men. "I found reading about, and talking to, male leaders was most helpful," she says. "It helped me learn how leadership is developed. When I joined a law firm, I read about men who were in law firms. When I became a judge, I talked to men who were judges. I read about Adam Clayton Powell, Leon Higginbotham, and Thurgood Marshall—people I admired or knew were famous." Powell was a U.S. Congressman and civil rights leader, Higginbotham was a prominent U.S. Judge and civil rights advocate, and Marshall was the first African American U.S. Supreme Court Justice.

"I tried to figure out what I had in common with them," Frederica says, "what there was about them that was applicable to me." There are some who might say, "a lot." Like those men, Frederica has risen to leadership heights in her profession. As President Judge of the Court of Common Pleas of Philadelphia, she has presided over medical malpractice and product liability cases, complex commercial litigation, and personal injury matters. Before becoming a judge, she practiced corporate and civil litigation with a major Philadelphia law firm. She also worked with the Senate of Pennsylvania as Chief Counsel of the Senate Insurance and Business Committee.

A college education was a foregone conclusion when Frederica was growing up. "I always knew I was going to college," she says. "It was the first priority of both of my parents. There was no question about it. Once I got to college, I knew I wanted to go forward with post-graduate education. But I still didn't know what career I wanted."

Frederica was a political science major, and had to make a decision about her future in her junior year. "I could get a PhD in political science," she says and pauses, "or go to Plan B." Law school was Plan B. "My parents challenged me to think about the law," she says.

Frederica never looked back. She always looked forward. "Growing up, I never saw myself as a judge," Frederica says. "But over the years, I tried to be thorough in everything I did. I tried to be prepared for whatever circumstances confronted me.

"You have to remember that if you make a statement, somebody will challenge it. You have to feel self confident about the work that you do."

Clearly, Frederica is self-confident. She learned a lot from the successful men she studied.

FRANCINE McNAIRY

" **Some people will say I mapped out a plan to get to where I am. But, really, my career evolved as I evolved. Every time I took a new position, I said, 'Let the chips fall where they may.'** "

– FRANCINE G. McNAIRY
President
Millersville University of Pennsylvania
Millersville

She has enjoyed many successes in a long and illustrious career in academia. Yet Francine McNairy still talks about what would happen when she made mistakes back in elementary school. "I played the violin, growing up in Pittsburgh," she explains. "We had the same conductor in the all-city orchestra from elementary through senior high school. We would be playing this wonderful song, and suddenly someone would hit a wrong note—loud.

"The conductor would stop us. He would not get angry. He just would say, 'You made a mistake. Now, stand up and take a bow.' And then we'd continue playing."

Francine has not been afraid to make a mistake since then. "Okay, so it was a doozy," she says. "You can take a bow, then get on with your life."

Not that she's made many mistakes, mind you. She didn't become the first female African American President of Millersville University of Pennsylvania, with oversight of a $100 million budget; one thousand employees; and eight thousand students, by hitting a lot of wrong notes.

Francine always knew she would go to college. "But that was the extent of my vision," she says. She entered a master's program in social work immediately after graduating from college. Although she had had no career goals until then, after spending all those years in college, she "decided to work in a college environment."

The opportunity to do so arose after she had worked as a social worker for three years. She heard that Clarion State College (now Clarion University of Pennsylvania) wanted to diversify its faculty and counseling center. She applied, and got a job as a counselor.

"I went to this predominantly white, rural town. It had a Kentucky Fried Chicken and a Burger King," she recalls. "I'm a city girl. I needed theaters and malls. But it would allow me to get my foot in the door, to work in a college environment. I decided to give it two years." She stayed for fifteen. Francine left Clarion to take a job as Associate Provost of West Chester University of Pennsylvania, and later became Acting Provost there, then moved on to become Provost at Millersville, considered one of the top regional public institutions of higher learning. Nine years later, she reached the pinnacle. She became President of the university, its Chief Executive Officer.

"Some people will say I mapped out a plan to get to where I am," Francine says. "But, really, my career evolved as I evolved. Every time I took a new position, I said, 'Let the chips fall where they may.'"

After all, if worse came to worse, she would stand up, take a bow, and then get on with her life.

> "I always wanted to do something in my culture, something in Spanish, but in the American way."

— MARITZA I. MENDOZA
President and CEO
The Mendoza Group, Inc.
Chester

The *"eureka!"* moment came as Maritza Mendoza waited in an airport in Puerto Rico for her flight back to Philadelphia from a business trip. "I was just sitting there, looking around," she recalls. "I kept seeing beautiful people walk by, attractive people, smiling people. It wasn't the kind of image the media usually portrayed of Latinos—uneducated and poor. I wished that the world could see Latinos the way I was seeing them at that moment.

"I had just a germ of an idea, and I jotted it down on a napkin, which turned into two, then three," she says. "If I could educate corporate America, because that's where there's the biggest impact, then I could make a difference."

Maritza—whom everyone knows as Mia—grew that germ of an idea into a groundbreaking business. She created the Mendoza Group, a full-service marketing and advertising agency that specializes in marketing to the Latino community. It's the first and only full-service agency committed to the Latino business community in the Philadelphia area.

Born in Panamá, she is the daughter of a Cuban mother and a Puerto Rican father who served as a military attaché to the U.S. Embassy in Bogotá, Colombia, Mia grew up in Puerto Rico, Colombia, and Panamá. She began her career in the broadcasting industry in August 1975, as host of *Tertulia,* the first Spanish-speaking talk show, which aired in Tampa

Bay, Florida. Later, Mia worked for CBS Sports as the interpreter for Latin American sports broadcasts to the United States before joining the Fox Network in Philadelphia. There, Mia formally entered the Latino marketing field after joining the Telemundo Network affiliate as Director of Programming and Sales Development. In an airport in Puerto Rico, on business for Telemundo, she first conceived the idea of an advertising agency that would reach out to Latino consumers specifically.

"I always wanted to do something in my culture, something in Spanish, but in the American way," Mia says. "What I came up with was entrepreneurial —a way to fill a need that I always saw but didn't put all together until I was in that airport, watching people.

"When I was little," she adds thoughtfully, "I always thought that I would grow up to be a teacher. I saw teaching as a way of helping people. I realize now I did live out what I wanted to do. What I teach is my culture."

The lesson to be learned from Mia's accomplishment is this: "If you look out there and find a need, you can fulfill it with what you know and what you love.

"My advice to young Latinos and Latinas is not to just daydream. *Dream!* I'm living my dream. And there's not one day that goes by that I don't love it."

RITA MURILLO

> **"When I was in high school, I wanted to be an attorney. I did everything I could do to talk. I went out for debate and forensics. I loved to talk, to express myself."**

— RITA MURILLO
Assistant Public Defender
Allegheny County Juvenile Division
Professed member
Congregation of the Sisters of Saint Joseph
Pittsburgh

She's a member of a religious order. She hangs out with juvenile delinquents. What's wrong with this picture? Not a thing if you're Sister Rita Murillo. As a member of the Congregation of the Sisters of Saint Joseph, Sister Rita, as she's known, says she is compelled to help the unfortunate. She does that by defending them in court. "I can be a voice for children who have no voice," she says. "Their lives are so tragic. I try to help them make choices so they can get along, even succeed, in the world."

Rita joined the religious order after graduating from high school, and taught Spanish in Pittsburgh high schools for many years. But eventually, she says, "I got bored. Much as I enjoyed it, it wasn't enough."

Although her religious calling won out, she had considered going to law school at one time. "When I was in high school, I wanted to be an attorney," she says. "I did everything I could do to talk. I went out for debate and forensics. I loved to talk, to express myself."

Eighteen years after becoming a religious, as she is called (only women who are cloistered are called nuns), Sister Rita enrolled in law school and became a public defense lawyer. She has worked in the federal and state court systems, and currently works in the Allegheny County juvenile court system.

"It was like going back to the fundamental desire I always had," she says of her decision to become a lawyer. "I always wanted the opportunity to plead the case for someone else.

"The vast majority of delinquents have no hope," she says. "They have such despair. I take each one and tell them there is another choice. It might be a small one, but one small choice will help them make better life choices.

"I just had a case of a young woman who beat and robbed an elderly woman. It was a terrible case. A psychiatrist who examined her said that she was a psychopath, that she didn't have a conscience.

"That was not my experience in talking with her. I pushed the court to authorize another evaluation. The second psychiatrist said she had a lot of problems, but he thought she could change."

The young woman successfully served time in a high-security facility for girls, entered a step-down program and completed it early, got a job as a night supervisor at a convenience store, and enrolled in college.

"Don't think that anything is impossible," says Sister Rita. "If you have a dream, you can follow it. There's usually a way."

ANA NÚÑEZ

> "Being involved in all those activities was really important in terms of my career. I learned to work with people, I developed self confidence, and I understood how teams operated."

— ANA ELIZABETH NÚÑEZ
Director, Center of Excellence of Women's Health
Director, Women's Health Education Program
Drexel University College of Medicine
Philadelphia

As a child, Ana Núñez says, "I was in touch with my inner geek. I used to get in trouble for having so many library fines. My sisters used to say, 'Stop reading. Go play.'" But she didn't. "I read all kinds of things that took me to other worlds," she continues. "The best way to get exposed to the world is through books. They can transport you to other universes, other possibilities. They open up things outside of your experience. That's very important. And you learn about yourself as you learn about other people."

Today, Ana Núñez is a renowned expert in women's health. As Director of the Women's Health Education Program at Drexel University College of Medicine in Philadelphia, she has developed new ideas and innovative programs that teach medical students about gender differences that they will encounter while practicing medicine. Her work has been replicated and adapted to enhance training in sex and gender medicine at other medical schools as well. Recognized as an expert nationally and locally, she has taught and advised thousands of medical students, residents, and women patients. And through the research that she spearheads as Director of the Women's Health Education Program, she has had a direct impact on hundreds of women participants.

Ana grew up in Altoona, the youngest of five children. She always was inquisitive and thirsty for knowledge, which led her to participate in a broad range of school and extra-curricular activities. In high school, she was involved in seventeen clubs and organizations, from teaching reading to elementary school children, to playing the violin in the school orchestra, from writing for the student newspaper, to being President of the student government.

"Being involved in all those activities was really important in terms of my career," she says today. "I learned to work with people, I developed self confidence, and I understood how teams operated.

"It was fun, but I realize now that I learned a whole lot about me, about what I'm good at doing—things I could apply in my career.

"Kids don't think about extra curricular activities as if they're a smorgasbord of possibilities for the future," she adds, "but they should.

"You never know what you're going to be good at until you try a lot of different things. Thinking of the possibilities is where you should be."

> "**People didn't know about Puerto Ricans in Kansas. All of a sudden, I was a minority. It was quite a shock to me.**"

— RAQUEL OTERO DE YIENGST
Vice Chair
Pennsylvania Human Relations Commission
Reading

It's hard to picture a tiny person like Raquel Otero de Yiengst creating as big a stir as she did. "My life has been very controversial," she admits. "I'm very small, but I don't back down. If I believe in something, I stand up for it." As far back as the 1960s, Raquel stood up to the Reading School Board and pushed for bilingual education for Latino children. Ultimately, she designed and implemented the Reading School District Transitional Bilingual Program for non-English speaking students.

As a result of her efforts on behalf of immigrant students, she was appointed by Governor Milton J. Shapp to the Pennsylvania Human Relations Commission more than twenty-five years ago. Although she retired from the school district, she remains on the Commission, and today is its Vice Chair. "It's another way to uphold the civil rights of all the citizens of Pennsylvania," she says.

Raquel grew up a privileged child in Puerto Rico. After graduating from private school there, she was sent to college in the United States—to a Catholic girls' school in Kansas. "I had nothing to do with the decision," she says. "My father didn't want me to go to school with boys.

"People didn't know about Puerto Ricans in Kansas. All of a sudden, I was a minority. It was quite a shock to me.

"I spoke very little English. It was very frustrating and very traumatic. I couldn't do my schoolwork the way I was accustomed to doing it, and I didn't get the grades I was accustomed to getting.

"Believe it or not, I think that was the reason that I am what I am today," she says. "I have devoted my entire life to the education of non-English-speaking students."

When she moved to Reading, Raquel quickly saw that the number of Latinos moving to the area was increasing rapidly. And she saw the Latino children struggling in school. It broke her heart.

"I saw these children sitting in classes, vegetating. I was really enraged," she says. "I thought, I have to do something for these children so they can be successful. I knew they had to learn English. English was the ticket to success."

Raquel and her ideas about bilingual education were not welcomed at first by the powers that be in Reading. Not a little bit. "They disliked me intensely," she says. "But it never bothered me, because I knew that what I was doing was the right and decent thing to do." Eventually, she prevailed. At the time of her retirement, the bilingual program she designed had educated more than one thousand students.

"I just hope," says Raquel, "that any girl who reads my story will realize that, as I've always said to the children I work with, 'If it is to be, it is up to me.'

"You cannot shun your responsibility," she says. "You have to do what you have to do."

> " I exposed myself to different things. I was like a vacuum cleaner, sucking in information. …Never did I ever think I would get a master's in public health. But it happened. It happened in a strange way. "

– CARMEN I. PARIS
Deputy Commissioner
Philadelphia Department of Public Health
Philadelphia

Carmen Paris has been a health-care professional for more than twenty years, but she has healed no one. "I am not a physician. I can't cure them, but I want to help them," she says. As Deputy Commissioner of the Philadelphia Department of Public Health, she does just that. She is responsible for coordinating and guiding every aspect of the department's Air Management Services to the Childhood Lead Poisoning Prevention Program, from the Medical Examiner's Office to Environmental Health Services. Carmen also oversees contract management for the city's nursing home and for Riverview health services.

She has been on a steady, upward path to the top of her field since she entered it, albeit a grueling path for this one-time welfare recipient and frazzled single parent.

Carmen was born and raised in Puerto Rico. "At thirteen," she says, "Carmen Paris didn't have a clue. I didn't know what I wanted to do when I grew up. I exposed myself to different things. I was like a vacuum cleaner, sucking in information. I thought maybe I would become a lawyer. Never did I ever think I would get a master's in public health. But it happened. It happened in a strange way.

"I came to America and I was on welfare," she explains. "I finally found a job with the City of Philadelphia as an applications clerk, which is a lower position than a clerk-typist. One of my colleagues died of HIV. It was in the early eighties. I had become friends with him. I even visited him in the hospital. But he never told me what he had. He was too embarrassed.

"I thought maybe we needed to tell people about diseases. I wondered, who does that? That's how my interest in public health grew," she says. "That's how I got here today."

Carmen had graduated from college in Puerto Rico, with a degree in education. Now, in America, she decided to get a graduate degree in public health. She was divorced from an abusive husband, raising a son, working, and studying and going to school at night.

"Was it difficult?" she asks. "Oh Lord," she answers. "Was it challenging?" she asks again. "Oh Lord," she answers again.

Carmen came to the Philadelphia Health Department as an AIDS educator while she was still in graduate school, "and worked my way up through the trenches.

"There were many challenges, many tears. But I never gave up. I knew that even if today is a bad day, it's a bad day that I don't have to live through again. Tomorrow I'm going to do my darnedest to see that it's better."

"**My parents owned several properties that they rehabbed. I remember dreaming that I would put three of them together and turn them into my clinic. It's unusual for a young person to think that big.**"

— ANA PUJOLS-McKEE
Chief Medical Officer and
Associate Vice President
Presbyterian Medical Center
University of Pennsylvania Health System
Philadelphia

Ana Pujols-McKee never thought small. Not when she was a child. And not now, as a physician and the highly esteemed administrator of a large medical center. "I always had a sense that I was not only going to be a doctor," she says, "but that I was going to run a big clinic. I'm not too far from the dreams that I had."

She certainly isn't. Ana holds a demanding administrative and leadership job as Chief Medical Officer of Penn Presbyterian Medical Center. She also continues to see patients, and is an Associate Professor of Medicine at the School of Medicine of the University of Pennsylvania.

Ana's parents came from Puerto Rico, and settled in the tough South Bronx when they were expecting Ana.

"My parents owned several properties that they rehabbed," Ana says. "I remember dreaming that I would put three of them together and turn them into my clinic.

"It's unusual for a young person to think that big," she admits. "But you're the maker of your dreams. It's not that important to know what you want to be. It's more important to be able to dream—and not have low ceilings in your dreams.

"If you want to dream of owning a restaurant, take that dream and say it's going to be a chain of restaurants. If you dream you're going to work

in a hospital, it's okay to say I'm going to run the hospital—because if you stop at working in the hospital, there are a whole lot of possibilities you're going to miss."

If Ana's high school guidance counselor had had her way, Ana would have missed the opportunity to go to college. "It still hurts me to know that my high school counselor rejected me many times when I asked for information about college," Ana says today. "I knew I would go, but I saw her as my resource. I kept going to see her, and she kept telling me to come back another time.

"One day I arrived at her office, and she jumped up and said, 'No, no, I'm having a meeting.' There was a group of students—none of color—meeting with a man in a suit. He said, 'Please bring her in. I'm interested.'" The man in the suit was from the State University of New York, from which Ana subsequently graduated.

"I learned a very important lesson that day," she says. "I learned not to accept rejection. I love the expression, 'Keep your eyes on the prize.'"

Today, Ana's eyes are on yet another prize. "I still dream," she says. "I'm very interested in building a health-care delivery system in an underdeveloped community or country. That's what I want to try next.

"It will happen," she says. "It will."

"**I was always troubleshooting, making the phone calls, because my mother didn't speak English. I learned to navigate the system.**"

— MARIA QUIÑONES-SÁNCHEZ
Regional Director
Puerto Rico Federal Affairs Administration
Philadelphia

Maria Quiñones-Sánchez has a big mouth. She always did and she always will. It's a good thing, too. It's why she has made such remarkable contributions to the Latino community in the past. And it's how, undoubtedly, she will continue to do so in the future."I was always tough and outspoken," Maria says. "I got smacked in the mouth a lot, but I kept on being outspoken.

"When I was young, I didn't understand the power of that kind of confidence, of being able to say what you wanted. Now I know that people do listen. When you can talk it and walk it, people take note of that." Maria walks and talks Latino empowerment."Life has given me these issues," she says. "My work is based on my life experiences."

As Regional Director of the Puerto Rico Federal Affairs Administration (PRFAA), Maria represents the government of Puerto Rico in all business, political, and economic exchanges between companies in Puerto Rico and in her territory, which comprises Pennsylvania, Delaware, and West Virginia. Among her accomplishments is a voter-registration drive, which resulted in more than twenty thousand new Latino voters.

Maria also has political aspirations. She ran for a Philadelphia City Council seat in 2003. She lost, but is considering running again in 2007. If elected, she would be the first Latina on Council.

Her career is a natural progression from her childhood in the Hunting Park section of Philadelphia. "I was always troubleshooting, making the phone calls, because my mother didn't speak English," Maria says. "I learned to navigate the system. I did it for my family, friends, and neighbors, too. Whenever anyone was buying a house or something like that, they came to me. People would ask, 'Whom do I call?' Once I learned something, it was recorded in my brain."

Her first job was with the Hunting Park Community Development Corporation. By the age of seventeen, she was its fiscal officer with direct oversight of its half-million-dollar budget. She served in several city government positions, including Deputy Commissioner of Elections and Legislative Assistant to two members of City Council, working on critical neighborhood projects.

Before joining PRFAA, Maria became the first female and youngest Executive Director of ASPIRA, Inc. of Pennsylvania, the largest Latino educational institution in Pennsylvania. Among other things, she oversaw the creation of the first bilingual charter school in Pennsylvania, Eugenio Maria de Hostos Community Charter School.

Her leadership roles on behalf of the Latino community come easily to Maria. "When you grow up with two older brothers like I did," she says, "you learn to defend yourself. You become tough."

> **"I decided as an adolescent that I wasn't going to be what the racists talked about when they said blacks don't work hard."**

— ESTELLE B. RICHMAN
Secretary
Pennsylvania Department of
Public Welfare
Harrisburg

Estelle Richman is nothing if not resilient. How else to explain her ability to go forward and fulfill her potential? And in a career of public service, she has worked tirelessly to help others do the same.

As Secretary of Pennsylvania's Department of Public Welfare, Estelle is unwavering in her quest to break down barriers to services for the state's most vulnerable citizens. Her efforts have resulted in a better-coordinated system of delivery that ensures that services for Pennsylvania children, adults, and families are provided effectively and efficiently. Before working her way to the top of the Public Welfare Department, she served as Philadelphia's first female Managing Director, and its first Health Commissioner. As Health Commissioner, she played a major part in the creation of a first-of-its-kind agency that transformed the system through which Philadelphia's low-income residents access mental health and substance-abuse services, providing a broad safety net for those most in need.

Estelle credits her upbringing for the determination and compassion that are the hallmarks of her public-service career. She grew up in Lynchburg, Virginia. "It was a very, very segregated world," Estelle says. As a child, she once was denied service at a whites-only lunch counter. "I was devastated," she says. "I thought I had done something wrong.

"Although my parents were both professionals, everything around us told us we were inferior—we had our own restrooms, we had to sit in the balcony at the movies. My parents told me, 'You will only be okay if you exceed everyone's expectations.'

"I decided as an adolescent that I wasn't going to be what the racists talked about when they said blacks don't work hard. You heard that when I was growing up. I thought, 'They can't mean me.' I was going to disprove what they said about us. I worked harder than everyone. I stayed later than everyone."

Although she has made it to the upper echelons of Philadelphia and Pennsylvania government, she still is not safe from racism; it still rears its ugly head on occasion.

She tells this story: "I had just moved to Philly and went down to have my utilities turned on," she recalls. "I filled out the form and turned it in. The lady said, 'You didn't put your welfare number on here.'

"Sometimes people make judgments. They think, 'A black person comes in, she must be on welfare.' I was the area Director of the Department of Welfare at the time."

The incident might have sent some into a nosedive. But not Estelle Richman. She remained philosophical. "All of us have a level of resiliency that lets us recover from life's pitfalls," she says. "You just need a sense of self-reliance, a sense of feeling good about yourself."

> "You just have to dare to dream how you want to be in the future."

— GRACE ROBINSON
General Agent
State Farm Insurance
Pittsburgh

I remember the day I first dared to dream," Grace Robinson says. "I remember exactly." Grace was ten or eleven, and she went to work with her mother. "My mom cleaned a pool hall," Grace says. "She was paid ten dollars a day. She was scrubbing to feed her kids. That's what Mom had to do. I never let her see me cry. I vowed I would help my mom and rise above it. I dared to dream of a big house, a big car. I dared to dream of owning a business."

No one was surprised by her dreams, or doubted that they would come true. Her grandfather would take young Grace with him wherever he went. "That one," he'd say, pointing to Grace, "that's the one who's going to be something someday." It just goes to show that it takes one to know one.

"My grandfather was the first entrepreneur in my family," Grace says. "He made a school bus out of a logging truck and drove kids to school." Grace was the first African American woman in Western Pennsylvania to own and operate a State Farm Insurance Agency. She took the job of an agent with no accounts, and grew it into a business with over two thousand households.

Born and raised in rural Toddtown, Alabama, Grace saw how hard her family worked, and was inspired by it.

Today, Grace is a leader in the male-dominated field of insurance. It hasn't been—it still isn't—easy.

"A woman in the workplace today still faces a glass ceiling," she says. "Women still have to work harder and prove themselves more than a male —for less pay. And an African American woman has a double whammy.

"But you don't use that as a crutch. To be successful, you have to run the race, stay the course, jump over the hurdles. You need to press on. You just have to dare to dream how you want to be in the future."

Grace helps others dare to dream, too. She founded Tomorrow's Future, Inc., a mentoring, entrepreneurial, and job-training program for teens. Its mission is to equip young people with basic communication and employment skills—everything from business writing to dressing for success—needed to compete in today's marketplace.

"Kids need to understand that education is what's going to speak for them," Grace says. "It will travel with them the rest of their lives. I tell kids, 'Take advantage of schooling. You'll see the rewards.'

"I'm seeing the rewards now."

"I had to start to think inside the box. I had to start thinking about my body, my mind, and my own spirituality. I had to start thinking about my future."

– ARGO L. SIMPKINS
Founder, President, and CEO
ABO Haven, Inc.
Philadelphia

In the beginning, Argo Simpkins's life was bleak. "I came up poor, not thinking much of myself," she says. "I had dark skin, and back then, back in the sixties, that was considered inferior. It's sad. It's crazy. I believed what people said, because I thought so myself." Then things got worse. "I was not very smart about life when I was young. I was a teen mother. I got pregnant at fifteen," she says. "When I started bringing big mistakes like that home, I woke up. I said, 'Get it together, girl. Your friends are getting addicted to drugs and you're pregnant.'

"I had to start to think *inside the box*," she says. "I had to start thinking about my body, my mind, and my own spirituality. I had to start thinking about my future."

Argo finished high school. "There was no expectation that I'd go to college," she says. "It wasn't until I got older that I found out I was intelligent. As I got older, I started thinking about things, putting things together."

Argo enrolled in CETA, part of the Comprehensive Employment and Training Act, a federal program in the seventies that trained youth for employment. Eventually, she worked for Campus Boulevard Corporation (CBC), a nonprofit workforce development organization. In nine years, she worked her way up from instructor to chief operating officer. Then she founded ABO (Abundantly Blessed Organization) Haven, Inc. and took over CBC.

ABO Haven, Inc. provides workforce development training and placement for low income, under educated people. It also operates a childcare center for its clients and others in similar circumstances. Argo says most of ABO Haven's graduates are working and contribute millions of dollars to Pennsylvania's economy.

Argo has devoted her professional life to helping young people avoid the mistakes she made herself.

"You have to understand that today is your future," she tells them. "You must think about tomorrow, because tomorrow is today. I didn't understand it then. I understand it now."

Argo also urges youngsters to find God. "Regardless of what religion you are," she says, "you need to know there is a real God. Learn that early. It can help you keep from making a lot of mistakes.

"You need to understand that what you put into life, and the way you treat people, is what you're going to get out of life and the way people are going to treat you. And you have to understand that the only person who can make you fail is you."

"**I was a teenage mother, but I got through it. So what? There's nothing I can't endure.**"

— SUSAN SLAWSON
Commanding Officer
Police Athletic League
Philadelphia

Susan Slawson doesn't want girls to emulate her. That's an odd perspective for a woman who, by any standard, is considered a role model today. A single, teenage mother, she was "naïve and ignorant," she says. "I didn't realize the actions you take now will determine what you're going to be doing ten years from now."

But Susan pressed on. She worked hard to finish high school. "Not finishing school was not something you could do in my family," she says. After high school, Susan worked for a bank. She decided to become a police officer because, she says, she wanted to help her community, and because, as a single mother, she wanted more job security.

Over the years, Susan rose through the ranks of the male-dominated police department. Today, she is the Commanding Officer of the Police Athletic League (PAL) of Philadelphia—the first African American woman to hold that job. The nonprofit organization serves at-risk boys and girls between the ages of six and eighteen with supervised environments where they can participate in athletic, recreational, and educational programs. Susan also created a Positive Images Program, which gives girls opportunities they might not have otherwise, including field trips to cultural institutions and meetings with successful businesswomen. In addition to her duties at PAL and as a single, working mother, Susan also found time to get her bachelor's degree in

management during the nineties, and now is working toward her graduate degree in psychology. Susan's assignment to PAL caps a remarkable career of service, which began as a beat cop in South Philadelphia, where she was proud to bring a woman's touch to the community.

"I'm not one of those women who think we are the same as men," she says. "I don't think I'm as physically strong as a man. If I'm going into battle, I'm not taking a woman with me. Men are here for a reason.

"But women bring balance, which the police department needs."

Susan earned the rank of Sergeant and then Lieutenant. Before being assigned to PAL, she was Commanding Officer in the Public Affairs Unit, where she served as the primary spokeswoman for the entire department.

If there's anything about her life story that young girls can benefit from, Susan says, it is the fact that even the most serious pitfalls need not be devastating. "I was a teenage mother, but I got through it," she says. "So what? There's nothing I can't endure. Kids need to know that life is not easy. They need to know they should expect pitfalls. But they also need to know they can survive."

"I was always looking up at the sky. My friends made fun of me. Everyone thought I was crazy."

— CAROLE I. SMITH
President and CEO
Workforce 2000 Initiative
and DigitalSistas.net
Executive Director
Mayor's Commission on Technology
Philadelphia

As a pre-teen, Carole Smith dreamed about going into space. "I was always looking up at the sky," she says. "My friends made fun of me. Everyone thought I was crazy. There wasn't even a space race yet. But I read comic books—Flash Gordon—and fairy tales. I read about everything that was fantastic and different."

As unconventional as her dreams were, Carole never even thought of doing anything with computers. Now *that* really would have been far out! Computers were virtually unheard of in Carole's reading experience.

Fast-forward. Carole's professional life now centers on computers. She is President and CEO of Workforce 2000, a nonprofit business she founded. It develops and implements computer-related training programs for African American youth and adults. Carole also founded DigitalSistas.net, an online network of African American women in technology and new media, and is the Philadelphia coordinator for Black Family Technology Awareness Week, a national program. In addition, she writes a column about technology for *The Neighborhood Leader*, a community newspaper in North and West Philadelphia; is host of a weekly radio program, *Carole's Corner on Technology*, on WURD 900 AM; and is producer, editor, and host of a monthly webcast/cable television program, Philadelphia's Got IT, which airs on three cable channels and 24/7 on the Web.

Carole is credited with focusing Philadelphia on the importance of technology in shaping the twenty-first century economy. She has served under two mayors as the Executive Director of the Mayor's Commission on Technology.

Her work is fantastic, yet precise, carefully designed to give African Americans the skills to compete in today's marketplace. It began when she read a U.S. Department of Labor report on the future of the U.S. economy and workers in the twenty-first century.

"The report said that unless specific policy changes were made, African Americans would do worse than they ever had before," she recalls, "because technology was going to be driving the economy, and they were behind the curve when it came to learning the necessary skills to work in that field.

"I started educating myself, learning about this, that, and the other. I decided that for the well-being of my race, I needed to help African Americans develop the skills they needed to succeed."

In a way, her technology-oriented career is ironic. "I'm the most non-technical 'technical' person around," she says. "Technology is not my forte. But, actually, that's good. I de-mystify it for them. I make ideas understandable."

In another way, however, her career is not at all ironic. "I always planned on being self-employed," she says. "I got pregnant in my last year of high school, but I went back and graduated after my daughter was born. It never made a difference in the way I saw myself. I knew I would graduate from high school and college, and I did; I knew I would go into business, and I did. I've always been strong-willed. If I want to do something, it will get done."

> " I was a great marbles player. My marble could spin better than anyone else's. It was my way of being competitive. My mother always told me that competitiveness spells success. "

– CECILE M. SPRINGER
President
Springer Associates
Pittsburgh

She was an environmentalist before the word was coined. She helped develop a new drug that was made into an over-the-counter product. She became an expert on subsidized housing, poverty, and accessibility for the handicapped.

But at the moment, Cecile Springer wants to talk about her marbles-playing skill as a child. "I was a great marbles player," she says. "My marble could spin better than anyone else's. It was my way of being competitive. My mother always told me that competitiveness spells success."

Today, Cecile is a consultant specializing in corporate and philanthropic programs. She became a consultant after retiring from the Westinghouse Electric Corporation, where she worked for many years, first as a manager engaged in nuclear energy and eventually as President of the Westinghouse Foundation, managing the portfolio of contributions made by the corporation.

Cecile has had a long and impressive career that spans more than fifty years—with no end in sight. Here is how she describes her career path:

"I always was one of the brightest in my class," she says. "I got my bachelor's and master's degrees in chemistry. But I still had lots of questions. So I went for another master's. I wanted to know how political decisions were made, especially in urban communities, because I could see that some streets were paved and others weren't, some schools were producing bright kids and some schools in other neighborhoods were not."

Of course, there's a lot more to the story than that. Cecile was born in New York City during the Great Depression. Her father was from Panamá, her mother from Barbados. They came to America for the opportunities it afforded. "To get an education and to become competitive meant success," Cecile says.

At only her second job out of graduate school, at a pharmaceutical company, she was part of a team that discovered a new drug that was successfully marketed. Shortly after that, she moved to Pittsburgh as a bride and worked for the University of Pittsburgh's Graduate Department of Biochemistry and Nutrition, which resulted in a number of publications on the biological degradation processes in animals.

After a brief stint as a stay-at-home mother, Cecile earned a master's degree in urban and regional planning, and then worked as an environmental planner. Soon, she realized she could put all of her talents together to create a new specialty, and went to work for Westinghouse.

"I was a physical scientist and a land-use policy person," she says. "Put those together and I was an 'environmentalist,' which wasn't even a word yet. I was better prepared than anyone to manage a new arena that would affect everyone in the U.S. I had all this information," she says. "I was the only one, from an environmental standpoint, who said nuclear power was safe. People who were very anti-nuclear would challenge me, but I could always out-argue them."

Cecile's mother was right. Competitiveness does spell success. It also spells Cecile.

— DAWN STALEY
Coach, Women's Basketball Team
Temple University
Philadelphia

Some people wear their hearts on their sleeve. Dawn Staley hangs it on the door of her office. "You have to do what you don't want to do to get what you want," the black and white letters on the sign read.

"That's the quote I live my life by," Dawn says. "It's simple, and everyone can understand it. Every aspect of every situation in life is covered. The idea is, if you have big goals, you're going to have to do the little things in order to achieve them."

Dawn—an all-American college basketball player; a three-time Olympic gold medal winner; a professional player; and the coach of Temple University's championship women's basketball team—didn't always live by those words.

"I wasn't one that liked to study, I didn't like to practice my sport," she says. "And I didn't always want to listen to the authority figures that told me to study and practice. I didn't hear that quote about 'doing what you have to do' until I was twenty-two. Then, everything fell into place."

Dawn grew up in the projects of North Philadelphia. She began playing basketball with the boys in her neighborhood as a way of staying out of trouble. A product of Philadelphia public schools, she led her high school to three straight public-league championships, then went on to become a three-time Kodak All-American at the University of Virginia. Dawn played with a number of professional teams abroad, before winning her first gold medal as a member of the first "Dream Team," which was comprised of professional women basketball players. She subsequently won two more gold medals, and is one of only three American women in history to win three in a row for basketball.

Today, Dawn is an All-Star player for the WNBA's Houston Comets, and, as Temple's women's basketball coach, is well on her way to shaping the program into a national powerhouse.

And, through her Dawn Staley Foundation, which has after-school and summer activities, she tries to inspire inner-city youth.

"Above all," she says, "I tell them to voice their concerns, talk to as many people as possible about what they want. You never know who can lend a helping hand." Dawn knows how hard that is to do.

"In my first year of college," she says, "I found that the academic part was really challenging. I questioned whether I could do it. Being shy, I wasn't really comfortable telling people what was going on, or asking for help. I'm one to try to get it done on my own. I had to step outside of myself and speak up."

That's what she urges young girls to do, too. "Kids don't talk a whole lot," she says. "A lot of them are shy like I was. That's why, when I see kids who are willing to put themselves on the line and express what's on their mind, I have a soft spot in my heart for them."

> **"I always knew I wanted to be a doctor. But knowing I wanted to be a doctor was different than knowing what it took to be a doctor."**
>
> — SUSAN C. TAYLOR
> Director
> Society Hill Dermatology
> Philadelphia

You may have caught her on national news shows like *Good Morning America* or *Today*, or seen her quoted in a newspaper or magazine. Maybe you've read her book, *Brown Skin: Dr. Susan Taylor's Prescription for Flawless Skin, Hair, and Nails* (HarperCollins). Susan Taylor pops up everywhere, it seems.

An internationally recognized expert in dermatology and ethnic skin disease, Susan frequently is interviewed by medical reporters. A private practitioner in Philadelphia, she specializes in the enhancement of the skin's appearance. But it is as Director of the Skin of Color Center at Saint Luke's Roosevelt Hospital Center in New York City, that Susan really has made her mark. She is responsible for patient care, grant writing, conducting clinical trials, and teaching at the first-of-its kind institution.

Born and raised in Philadelphia, Susan is a University of Pennsylvania and Harvard-trained physician. "I always knew I wanted to be a doctor," she says. "But knowing I wanted to be a doctor was different than knowing what it took to be a doctor.

"In some respects it's a lot easier for kids today," she says. "They have the Internet. They can use it to get all sorts of information. When I was growing up, I depended on talking to people along the way—family members, neighbors, professors, and teachers."

Susan has never hesitated to tap other people—even people she didn't know—to develop the knowledge and skills she needed.

Take the Skin of Color Center, for example. "I was talking to one of my former professors about developing a separate field focusing on skin of color," she recalls, explaining there are racial and ethnic differences when it comes to disease appearance and response to treatment among African Americans, Latinos, and Asians. There also are issues relating to cultural habits and beliefs.

"We decided there was a need for a center specifically for people of color," she says. "Nothing like this had ever been done. And what the professor said to me was, 'Okay, Susan, create one.'

"Now, some would be frightened by that," she says. "To me, it was exciting. Others would say, 'I don't know how to do it.' But I knew what we wanted to achieve. So I set about talking to everyone I could find. People I didn't know. Professionals with all sorts of expertise. I was able to draw upon their knowledge and experience to help me form the Center."

It's something youngsters can do when it comes to figuring out their futures, Susan believes.

"Don't be afraid to talk to someone you don't know," she says. "You'd be very surprised. You can introduce yourself and she will talk to you. I get emails all the time from kids interested in dermatology. I always have them come talk to me. I help them plot out strategy. I'm happy to do it."

> # "The real challenge is not to use your color or your socio-economic circumstances as an excuse. You have to make those things work for you."

– JUDITH A.W. THOMAS
Dean
School of Social Sciences and Behavioral Studies
Lincoln University of Pennsylvania
West Chester

She is known fondly as "Dr. T" at Lincoln University. Clearly, Judith Thomas is much beloved. And why not? She reaps what she sows. "No one will approach you if you have a sour face," she says. "If you want people to trust you, you have to behave in a way that is trustworthy. You have to respect people if you expect them to respect you."

Born and raised in New Kensington, near Pittsburgh, Judith is Dean of the School of Social Sciences and Behavioral Studies at Lincoln University of Pennsylvania, the nation's first historically black college. She has been at Lincoln for more than thirty years, moving up from a professor to Chair of the Education Department and interim Vice President for Enrollment Planning and Student Life, before reaching the exalted position of Dean. Prior to joining the faculty at Lincoln, Judith taught English, Spanish, and debate in the Highlands School District in Natrona Heights, and was the first African American teacher in Natrona Heights. Her credentials include a bachelor's degree in English and Spanish, and a master's and Ed.D in education.

Despite all of her years as an educator, Judith says she has never stopped acquiring knowledge. "My philosophy, even today at one hundred years old," she says with tongue planted firmly in cheek, "is that I try to learn from everybody. There's always someone from whom I can learn something. People out there are doing things that are special, which I try to replicate in my own way."

The students at Lincoln obviously think Judith is pretty special herself. They voted her the "Most Dedicated Academic Dean." Of all of her many awards and honors, she says, that was among the most meaningful.

To be sure, life hasn't been all honors and accolades for Judith. "There was a lot of prejudice where I grew up," she says. "It was obvious from the way we were treated that people assumed if you were black, you were poor and illiterate.

"Unfortunately, racism is still alive and well today," she adds. "Everything in the media suggests that's so.

"Yes, society in general is better than it was. But you have to understand—bigotry is the reality. It's just something you have to overcome. The real challenge is not to use your color or your socio-economic circumstances as an excuse. You have to make those things work for you.

"You just have to keep on keeping on," she says. "You have to demonstrate what your strengths are and move forward."

Judith never was deterred by the bigotry she encountered. "I always said that one day people would read about me, that I would be somebody," she says. "I don't know if other people saw it in me, but my parents did. I was blessed with wonderful, caring parents."

> "Freedom of speech recognizes the responsibility that comes with that freedom. Take the high road. Be accountable. It serves no one any good to abuse the freedom we so dearly love and cherish."

— C. DELORES TUCKER
(1927 – 2005)
Civil Rights Activist
Philadelphia

Throughout her remarkable life, prominent civil rights activist C. DeLores Tucker, a champion of equal rights and of increasing the number of women in politics, was an inspiration to women and girls in Pennsylvania and across the nation. Although she died in 2005 at the age of seventy-eight, her life, her work, and the values that she stood for continue to galvanize those who loved and admired her.

Carole Smith, President and CEO of the Workforce 2000 Initiative, is one of them. "I remember the moment I first saw her," Carole says. "It was in 1970 and I was attending a conference in Philadelphia. I saw this woman at the front of the room, holding her own in a group of men. I saw how all those men were talking to her. They obviously had a great deal of respect for her.

"I said to myself, 'Well looky here,'" she says. "There just weren't women, much less black women, who had that kind of stature and commanded that kind of reverence. It truly was an inspiration."

C., as she was known, was the tenth of eleven children of Caribbean-born parents. Known for wearing colorful dresses with matching turbans, and for thunderous speeches evocative of her preacher-father, she first took to the stump when she was sixteen, protesting from the back of a flatbed truck outside of a Center City Philadelphia hotel that refused to accommodate African American athletes.

She strode onto the national scene in 1965, walking arm-in-arm with the Reverend Martin Luther King, Jr., and his wife Coretta Scott King, during the seminal civil rights march from Selma to Montgomery, Alabama.

In 1970, she became the first African American woman to be Vice Chair of the Pennsylvania Democratic Party, and the first woman Vice President of the Pennsylvania NAACP. One year later, she made history when she became the first black female to serve as Pennsylvania's Secretary of State. In that job, she helped streamline voter registration, spearheaded the move to lower the voting age from twenty-one to eighteen, and established the first Pennsylvania Commission on the Status of Women.

Later, C. became head of the minority caucus of the Democratic National Committee and a founding member of the National Women's Political Caucus. She also founded the National Political Congress of Black Women, now called the National Congress of Black Women, and created the Commission on Presidential Appointments, which she convened every four years no matter who the President was. Through the Commission, she promoted black women for appointed positions in every administration since 1984.

In the last decade of her life, C. became an outspoken critic of rap music's obscene, violent, and misogynic lyrics. She filed lawsuits and went to jail several times for picketing record producers. Although she was criticized by some as advocating censorship in urging that rap music be kept off the air, C. held to the principles that defined her life.

"Freedom of speech recognizes the responsibility that comes with that freedom," she told broadcasters. "Take the high road. Be accountable. It serves no one any good to abuse the freedom we so dearly love and cherish."

> "The path of learning how we can best benefit the Universe—because that's what we're here for—is different for everyone. Some people come here knowing; for others, it's a discovery process."

— CAROL SANDRA MOORE WELLS
United States Magistrate Judge
Eastern District of Pennsylvania
Philadelphia

Ralph Waldo Emerson's quote, "Once you make a decision, the Universe conspires to make it happen," resonates with Carol Wells. She wouldn't be where she is today—a U.S. Magistrate Judge and the first female African American jurist on the federal court in the Eastern District of Pennsylvania—if she hadn't been determined and open to a desired, yet unexpected, opportunity that led her ultimately to that position.

"The path of learning how we can best benefit the Universe—because that's what we're here for—is different for everyone," she says. "Some people come here knowing; for others, it's a discovery process."

For Carol Wells, it was a bit of both. Born and raised in the Tioga-Nicetown section of Philadelphia, Carol had a bachelor's degree in education and two years of law school when she left to get married and raise four sons. Teaching and parenting are noble undertakings, she says, "but were not all I was put here to do.

"I remember being home on a Saturday," she says. "I was ironing. I had four children, so there was a lot to do. I got a good set of motivational tapes to listen to, and I literally listened from morning to night.

"By the end of the day, I decided that the children were old enough, and I had waited patiently enough to go back and finish my last year of law school. I felt something was missing."

Carol finished law school and took temporary secretarial and paralegal jobs until finally landing a job as a litigator in a private law firm. It was just what she wanted to do. Or so she thought. An opposing lawyer in a case she handled asked if she had ever considered working in the City Law Department. "I said no," Carol recalls. "I wanted to work at a law firm. I wasn't thinking of the government at all."

Despite Carol's protestations, the lawyer urged her to be open-minded and began to enumerate the different departments that had job openings. "When he described the litigation department, my eyes lit up," Carol says. She pursued the job and "in three months, I had more in-court opportunities than I'd ever had at the law firm.

"Saying yes or no to an opportunity can affect your whole life," she says. In nearly ten years as a litigator in the City Solicitor's office, trying and settling dozens and dozens of civil cases in federal and state court, Carol rose from being an Assistant to Chief Assistant to Deputy Solicitor to Senior Attorney.

The judges in the federal district court in Philadelphia chose Carol to become a U.S. Magistrate Judge, a testament to the respect they had for her work ethic and legal mind.

"And to think," she says, "I would not be sitting on the bench today if it weren't for an attorney friend who embarked on a conversation that I at first resisted." Case closed.

"**Don't let the images you receive through the media drive who you are or what you want to become.**"

– KAREN FARMER WHITE
Vice President
Education and Community Resource Center
WQED Multimedia
Pittsburgh

Karen Farmer White is uncomfortable being called a role model. "Who am I?" she asks. "I was lucky." Maybe she was. But she certainly doesn't take that luck for granted. Her career centers on assuring that the benefits of her upbringing, her education, and her experience will help those less privileged than she.

"I was very fortunate growing up," she says. "My mother was a great role model for me. She had an undergraduate degree, a master's, and a doctorate. Imagine, pursuing school and a career while raising four children. My father did the same thing. He worked and went to college, and also got a doctorate."

Both of her parents were educators. Karen is, too—and more. As Vice President of Education for WQED Multimedia, she has created shows and gotten funding for projects that expanded the reach and influence of programming for pre-school and school-age children. Her focus is increasing the media literacy of today's youth, especially minority youth, by teaching them how to assess what they see on popular cultural outlets such as TV, the movies, and the Internet. "I'm continually learning about young people today," she says, "figuring out what they need, and trying to find ways to help them."

Karen has been doing that throughout her career. Before joining WQED, she was Executive Director of the Program to Aid Citizen Enterprise (PACE), responsible for overall operations, including two college-preparatory programs for minority youth. Karen also was responsible for the development of a program that provided training and technical assistance to community organizations.

The seeds of this passion for helping minority youth were sown early in her career, when Karen taught at a local community college.

"It was an eye-opener," she says. "What's happening in this world—how hard life is—is astounding. Kids today have all this media stuff coming at them. Everyone is marketing images of sexuality, which weren't there when I was coming up.

"That's why my big thing now is media literacy, helping young people understand that they can't believe everything they see and hear. Just because it's on the Internet or TV, it isn't necessarily true.

"I'm all about consumer education. Look at the ads for cigarettes. They project the idea that smoking is sexy. What is that about? It's about selling you a product that in the long run is harmful."

The lessons Karen teaches through the programming she provides are simple and straightforward—and life affirming.

"Try to be comfortable with who you are," is her message. "Don't let the images you receive through the media drive who you are or what you want to become. Don't be defined by media images.

"Kids have to learn this. It needs to be taught," she says. "It's as important as learning to read."

> "Everybody in my family had to learn to sing or play the piano. It was how we learned to be disciplined. What wasn't an option was not working to be the best you could be."

— DORIS CARSON WILLIAMS
President
African American Chamber of Commerce
of Western Pennsylvania
Pittsburgh

As a child, Doris Carson Williams was like a sponge. "I absorbed as much positive energy as I could," she says. "I was very observant. I had a great grandmother who gave beautiful parties with linens and crystal glassware. When I was around the people she entertained, I would listen to how they talked and what they said. I was putting all of it into context. You could say that I'm a product of my environment."

What Doris learned through those early observations was the ways of the business world. "I saw women who were well groomed, wearing suits, and carrying briefcases," she says. "I liked that image."

Today, Doris is a powerful advocate for African Americans and minority businesses. As the first President of the African American Chamber of Commerce of Western Pennsylvania, she promotes opportunities for African American business owners in the region through a variety of programs and services. Since opening the doors and establishing the Chamber's office, she has grown the organization from twenty members to over five hundred.

Doris grew up in Pittsburgh. Her parents worked for the University of Pittsburgh—her father as a janitor, her mother in human resources. They instilled in Doris the drive that propels her to succeed in whatever she does.

"Everybody in my family had to learn to sing or play the piano," she says. "It taught us to be disciplined.

"What wasn't an option was not working to be the best you could be. We celebrated our successes. You had to be in the race. You had to either win, place, or show.

"It's healthy to learn to compete," she says. "If you do the best you can, then you win no matter where you come out in the race. You could be number two. But that's better than number ten. And to be number one means you really have to work hard."

Working hard is what Doris is all about. So is working smart. "Girls are exceptionally skilled," she says. "We know how to work a situation to our advantage. It's that same skill that will allow you to be great. You never want to lose your ladylike, feminine qualities while striving to be the best you can be.

"It's okay to wear a dress. It's okay to look ladylike," she says. "And don't be afraid to make mistakes. What builds character is not making the same mistake twice."

ABOUT THE PENNSYLVANIA COMMISSION FOR WOMEN

The Pennsylvania Commission for Women was established by Executive Order of Governor Milton J. Shapp in 1974 to bring the laws of the Commonwealth into compliance with the Equal Rights Amendment. Its formation legitimized many concerns of the women's movement and brought them into the mainstream of the political process.

The Commission has evolved since its initial establishment. While still a vehicle for change, today's Commission is an ardent advocate for health care, business, and human rights legislation. It encourages the formation of County Commissions for Women and facilitates coalitions among women's organizations across the State. In keeping with its mission, the Commission continues to break down barriers, gain footholds, and empower the women of Pennsylvania. Governor Edward G. Rendell signed the most recent Executive Order on June 22, 2003, appointed twenty-eight members to the Commission, and named Leslie Stiles as Executive Director.

Among the Commission's initiatives are the annual Pennsylvania Governor's Conference for Women, legislative advocacy, a statewide multi-media marketing campaign to raise awareness of women's issues, the *Status of Pennsylvania Women* report, the PCW hotline, and the *Commonwealth of Women* newsletter.

PENNSYLVANIA COMMISSION FOR WOMEN

Marie A. Savard, M.D. (Chair), Montgomery County
Leslie Anastasio, Philadelphia County
Joyce M. Branche, Dauphin County
Francesca L. Cantarini, Philadelphia County
Bernadette S. Comfort, Indiana County
Thera Martin Connelly, Philadelphia County
Hon. Jacqueline R. Crahalla, Montgomery County
Susan Frietsche, Esq., Allegheny County
Amy Clothier Gaudion, Esq., Cumberland County
Melissa Weiler Gerber, Philadelphia County
Irene Horstman Hannan, Chester County
Marlene Gary Hogan, Esq., Allegheny County
Gail E. Kessler, Montgomery County
Donna L. Kreiser, Esq., Lancaster County
Betsy Bechtolt Magley, Allegheny County
Rebecca Martin, Erie County
Marciene S. Mattleman, Ed.D, Philadelphia County
Leslie Anne Miller, Esq., Montgomery County
Phyllis S. Mowery, Cumberland County
Lois Eisner Murphy, Esq., Montgomery County
Shawn Murphy, Luzerne County
Ho-Thanh Nguyen, Cumberland County
Carmen I. Paris, M.P.H., Philadelphia County
Susan G. Smith, Philadelphia County
Linda L. Stevenson, Erie County
Joanne Tosti-Vasey, Ph.D., Centre County
Judith Weinberger, Lackawanna County
Robin Wiessmann, Bucks County